Becoming
a WOMAN of
EXTRAORDINARY
Faith

JULIE CLINTON

HARVEST HOUSE PUBLISHERS
EUGENE, OREGON

BECOMING A WOMAN OF EXTRAORDINARY FAITH
Copyright © 2011 by Julie Clinton
Published by Harvest House Publishers
Eugene, Oregon 97402
www.harvesthousepublishers.com

Library of Congress Cataloging-in-Publication Data
   Clinton, Julie, 1961-
   Becoming a woman of extraordinary faith / Julie Clinton.
     p. cm.
   ISBN 978-0-7369-3926-3 (pbk.)
   ISBN 978-0-7369-4210-2 (eBook)
   1. Christian women—Religious life. I. Title.
   BV4527.C569 2011
   248.8'43—dc22

2011012150

Contents

Acknowledgments

It's in the quiet moments of my life that God has revealed so much of himself to me, and I praise him for his grace and faithfulness! I also want to extend a special note of appreciation to my circle of dear friends who encourage me in my faith walk…women whom I deeply admire and value as close friends.

Some of those women include Stormie Omartian, Carol Kent, Linda Mintle, Georgia Shaffer, Angela Thomas, Michelle McKinney Hammond, Lysa TerKeurst, Thelma Wells, Jennifer Rothschild, and Linda Barrick, who have come together to share their stories in the DVD portion of this Bible study. I really appreciate your honesty in sharing your heart and the time you've graciously given to help bring this project to life.

A special thank you to Pat Springle for his help in writing this book. God has blessed you with incredible insights and a heart that radiates the love of Christ. I also want to give special thanks to Dr. Joshua Straub and Laura Faidley for the editing expertise, research, and insight they provided throughout the entire book. You guys are amazing!

Extending a heartfelt and sincere thank you to Harvest House Publishers doesn't seem enough for the support and encouragement they have given me over the years, but here goes—thank you to Hope Lyda, Gene Skinner, Terry Glaspey, Bob Hawkins, and the entire Harvest House staff, for believing in the EW platform and message and allowing me the opportunity to share my heart with women around the world.

And of course, to the EW Team—thank you for dedicating long hours during the week and on the weekends to faithfully serve Christ and women across the nation. I am grateful and feel extremely blessed to serve with you.

Finally, to my husband, Tim, my daughter, Megan, and my son, Zach—I thank God every day for the blessing you are in my life. You mean more to me than anything in this world. I love the way you love me. Thank you for being you!

Week 1

Extraordinary Hope:
Breaking Through Fear and Doubt

*[hope:] a strong and confident expectation
that God is real, present, and working for my
good, even when life spins out of control*

American writer Jean Kerr perceived the essence of hope. She said, "Hope is the feeling you have that the feeling you have isn't permanent."[1] Hope is as essential to life as breath itself. We may exist without it, but we can't be truly alive unless, in the depths of our hearts, we are convinced that something good will come.

George Iles similarly observed, "Hope is faith holding out its hand in the dark."[2]

Hope is powerful and necessary, but it can be very slippery. False hopes lead to shattered dreams, and failure to hope at all results in perpetual apathy and isolation. What can we count on? What has God promised?

This week we'll look at Hannah, a woman who held on to hope during long years of disappointment when her hope remained unfulfilled. We'll also see how another woman found the true source of hope at an unguarded moment. Ultimately, our supreme hope isn't in the things we can see, taste, and feel. Our deepest longing is to find meaning and peace in our relationship with God himself.

Tenacious Hope

If I do not look with eyes of hope…
I know nothing of Calvary love.

AMY CARMICHAEL

There's nothing like a good hard cry, but for Hannah, tears were a daily reality. For years, this woman of God had prayed for a child, and still her arms were empty. When God doesn't "come through" the way we think he should, it's easy to become jaded. Bitter. To give up. However, Hannah chose to cling tenaciously to the hope that God was real, present, and working for her good.

In the Word

Read 1 Samuel 1 today and pay special attention to verses 10-11:

> *In her deep anguish Hannah prayed to the LORD, weeping bitterly. And she made a vow, saying, "LORD Almighty, if you will only look on your servant's misery and remember me, and not forget your servant but give her a son, then I will give him to the LORD for all the days of his life."*

Many of us live such frazzled lives as mothers that we long for a few minutes of peace and quiet to get away from all the noise and demands of our children—a warm, unhurried bath sounds like heaven! But I've talked to women who would give anything to face those demands. They feel terribly empty because they can't have children. Each day, they wake up to the reality of the hole in their hearts that simply can't be filled by anything else.

Hannah felt exactly the same way. In a story reminiscent of others we've read, her husband Elkanah had two wives, and the other wife, Peninnah, had several sons and daughters. In their culture, a woman's inability to conceive wasn't just a psychological blow; it was considered to be a sign of God's disapproval.

Elkanah, her husband, was a good and sensitive man. He loved Hannah with all his heart, and he honored her in every way he could. When he found her crying because she was so grieved, he asked, "Why are you weeping? Why don't you eat? Why are you downhearted? Don't I mean more to you than ten sons?" (Sounds just like a man!) He meant well, but Elkanah simply didn't understand the depth of her sorrow and shame.

The other woman in the family didn't match Hannah's husband's comfort and understanding. Jealousy goaded Peninnah to make fun of Hannah, and I'm sure Peninnah took every opportunity to talk about her children in front of her.

Hannah could have given up on her dream of having a child, but she didn't. Through her heartache, despite the ridicule she endured in her own home each day, and in the face of the shame she felt when she walked out in public, she kept asking God to answer her prayer. And after years of praying, pleading, and waiting, God gave her a son—but not just any son.

Little Samuel became a mighty prophet and anointed the first kings of Israel. Hannah's name means "grace" or "favor." God certainly rewarded her persistent hope with his favor.

Make It Real

Most women struggle with holding on to hope. Should we ever give up on our hopes? No one can answer that for us. Novelist Pearl Buck once commented, "Life without idealism is empty indeed. We must have hope as we must have bread; to eat bread without hope is still slowly to starve to death."[1] God's delay is not necessarily a definitive "no." It takes wisdom to tell the difference between his voice and our personal longings. Sometimes, God wants to provide a miraculous answer. The process of waiting and hoping purifies our motives, strengthens our faith, and prepares us to accept God's answer with gratitude.

What is something you've hoped for over a long period of time? Has God answered your prayer? Describe what happened and how it affected you.

Look over 1 Samuel 1 again. Describe Hannah's emotions and relationships in the years before Samuel was born. Do you think she regretted making her pledge to offer her child to God if he would give her a son? Why or why not?

How do you think we can discern the difference between God saying, "Keep hoping and waiting," and "No, it's not my will"?

How can you leave your heart open to the idea that God may answer differently than you expect?

Take a moment to read each one of these verses and think about how they apply to your life. Wherever you can do it, insert your name in the verses. Pray these passages over your heart.

- "But now, Lord, what do I look for? My hope is in you. Save me from all my transgressions...Hear my prayer, LORD, listen to my cry for help; do not be deaf to my weeping" (Psalm 39:7-8,12).

- "For you have been my hope, Sovereign LORD, my confidence since my youth. From birth I have relied on you; you brought me forth from my mother's womb...As for me, I will always have hope; I will praise you more and more" (Psalm 71:5-6,14).

- "But blessed is the one who trusts in the LORD, whose confidence is in him. They will be like a tree planted by the water that sends out its roots by the stream. It does not fear when heat comes; its leaves are always green. It has no worries in a year of drought and never fails to bear fruit" (Jeremiah 17:7-8).

Heart to Heart

One of my favorite quotations about hope is by Anne Lamott:

> Hope begins in the dark, the stubborn hope that if you just show up and try to do the right thing, the dawn will come. You wait and watch and work: you don't give up.[2]

Coming to God with a spirit of expectation gives us the freedom to live before God and others with deep joy, not anger, resentment, or bitterness...no matter what the outcome, no matter how long the walk. This is one of the most difficult journeys of a woman's heart. Our challenge is to cling tenaciously to hope the way Hannah did, but to realize that God sometimes says "no" instead of "keep trusting, hoping, and waiting."

Lord, give me hope in the areas of my life where I've quit believing that things could be any different. Give me wisdom to know the difference between my heart's hopes and your plans for me. Even when you say "no," God, I want to trust you.

Day 2

God Moments

*Hope fills the afflicted soul with such inward joy and
consolation that it can laugh while tears are in the eye, sigh
and sing all in a breath; it is called "the rejoicing of hope."*

WILLIAM GURNALL

Ever had a moment in your life when God caught you completely by surprise? You weren't necessarily looking for him, and maybe you hadn't even been praying, and then, out of nowhere, God steps in and does something.

I like to call these situations "God moments"—reminders that God is there for you and me. That he is always pursuing us with his love, even when we ignore him, get too busy, or even intentionally run away. For the Samaritan woman, going to the well became a God moment when a stranger asked for a cup of water…and that stranger turned out to be Jesus himself!

In the Word

Read John 4 today and pay special attention to verse 9:

> *The Samaritan woman said to him, "You are a Jew and I am
> a Samaritan woman. How can you ask me for a drink?" (For
> Jews do not associate with Samaritans.)*

She had tried to fill the hole in her heart with a man, but it didn't work out. The heartache she experienced caused her to long even more for intimacy, so she found another man. This one didn't work out, either, nor the next one, nor the next one, nor the next one. With each attempt, her longing for love turned into desperation to be wanted by some-body—anybody! Each of her choices seemed reasonable at the time.

After all, each man offered love, didn't he? But the pattern of broken relationships ruined her reputation and created a persona of shame and doubt. To avoid the catcalls of the other women, she went to the well to draw water in the middle of the day when no one else was around. Her hope for love had left her as "that woman."

But this day would be different. When she arrived at the well, a stranger was sitting there. "Good," she probably thought. "He doesn't know me." The man was a Jew, and since she was a Samaritan, she was sure he would ignore her. But he didn't. He initiated a conversation by asking politely, "Will you give me a drink?"

In the next few minutes, this stranger exposed her deepest sorrows and highest hopes. He spoke words of kindness and truth, but just as importantly, he communicated that he genuinely cared for her—in a very different way than the other men she had known! As he explained the answers to life's most important questions, she had been a little con-fused. He wasn't the least bothered by that. He kept explaining until she understood. I love that!

Suddenly, the hole in her heart was filled, and her hopes, which she had probably given up on long before, became a reality. She had come to the well that day with no thought of finding the answer to life's rid-dle. But there at the well, she found not only the theological answer, but the Savior who *is* the answer.

For years, she had longed for a relationship with someone who would accept her, and that day, she found someone who genuinely loved her and offered her more than she could imagine. How do we know that she "got it"? She went back to town and told everybody (the ones who had rejected her and mocked her, the ones she had been afraid of only hours before) that she had met the Christ, and they asked him to stay two more days to hear the message that changed her life.

Make It Real

Every woman's story is a little bit different. Hannah had pleaded with God for years to fulfill her hopes; the woman at the well didn't even know how to define her hope—but Jesus did. Sometimes, even when we've abandoned hope, God shows up in some way to touch our hearts with grace, comfort, and healing. Isn't that just like God? We quit. He never does.

What are some "God moments" in your life? Has God "shown up" unexpectedly to fulfill a long-cherished dream, either in your life or in the life of a friend or family member?

Look at John 4:1-30 again. What drives someone to be involved in serial, broken relationships? Why do you think this woman was open to Jesus that day?

How can we prepare our hearts so we're ready when God shows up in unexpected ways to fulfill our hopes?

Take a moment to read each one of these verses and think about how they apply to your life. Wherever you can do it, insert your name in the verses. Pray these passages over your heart.

- "But the eyes of the LORD are on those who fear him, on those whose hope is in his unfailing love. We wait in hope for the LORD; he is our help and our shield. In him our hearts rejoice, for we trust in his holy name" (Psalm 33:18-21).

- "Yet this I call to mind and therefore I have hope: Because of the LORD's great love we are not consumed, for his compassions never fail. They are new every morning; great is your faithfulness. I say to myself, 'The LORD is my portion; therefore I will wait for him'" (Lamentations 3:21-24).

Heart to Heart

So often, I am preoccupied with everything going on around me—getting Zach to his game, trying to catch up on laundry, or helping Megan study for her microbiology test. I'm running the world around my agenda so intensely that I fail to see and invite God into what I'm doing.

I've often settled for just "surviving" my day, rather than embracing it as an opportunity for me to see God moments. They aren't necessarily dramatic or miraculous, but they are wonderful reminders that God is with us, strengthening us and giving us enough grace for each step…each moment.

Lord, open up my eyes today to the "God moments" all around me. I want to see things the way you see them, and invite you into every part of my day—even the really ordinary parts. Meet me, God, where I least expect it.

Day 3

Shattered Dreams

Hope deferred makes the heart sick,
but a longing fulfilled is a tree of life.
PROVERBS 13:12

Everybody gets the blues sometimes. But persistent disappointment and frustration, or worse, betrayal, failure, and loss, can wither our hope and shatter our once-precious dreams. When depression becomes the norm in life, we struggle to just survive...and just get out of bed.

In the Word

Read Psalm 42 today and pay special attention to verse 5:

Why, my soul, are you downcast? Why so disturbed within me? Put your hope in God, for I will yet praise him, my Savior and my God.

Many women today live in a state of low-grade depression. The accumulation of their discouragements has gotten the best of them, and they have settled for a life of little joy, love, hope, or adventure. It's easy to begin to disengage—to no longer want to take risks, to make self-protection one's greatest goal.

For a long time, they hoped people would love them, their children would make great decisions, and friends would always come through—but somewhere along the way added disappointments tipped the scales, and they struggled to believe in those "good things." Few of them have ever articulated this conclusion, but their lifestyle of apathy and emptiness tells the whole story.

King Solomon observed it accurately: "Hope deferred makes the heart sick." A lot of women today are heartsick, and they're not even looking for a cure. Ever been around someone who is depressed? Have you ever been depressed?

I believe there are two distinct types of events that threaten our sense of hope. One consists of *authentic, normal desires for love, stability, and meaning in life.* We want our marriages, our families, and our friendships to be full of meaning and love. When these hopes are shattered, either by choices or by accidents, our hearts are broken.

In our darkest moments we feel alone, and we isolate ourselves even more from those who really care about us. Yes, we sometimes need to be alone, but not all the time. We don't want to bore or bother anyone with our grief, but we sometimes fail to realize that some people really want to come alongside and help us get through these difficult days. It is, in fact, their gift and privilege to help us in this way.

The other threat to our sense of hope is more insidious: *When unrealistic expectations are shattered*, we don't grieve. Instead, we can become resentful. We live in a wealthy culture, and we take incredible conveniences for granted. We complain if the air conditioning isn't perfect, or if the plane is a few minutes late.

Only a generation or two ago, air conditioning was a novelty for only the wealthiest, and travel was measured in days and weeks, not minutes and hours. But we've gotten used to conveniences like microwave ovens, drive-thru windows, instant this and quick that, and some of us feel genuine resentment if our desires aren't met—perfectly and instantly!

Our solution is to try to do more things more quickly, multi-tasking and text messaging our lives away. The more we trust technology to smooth our lives and make us happy, the more we risk becoming distracted, missing the people we pass by, and becoming annoyed by any inconvenience. The remedy in this case isn't grieving with friends; it's getting a fresh look at what's most important in our lives.

Make It Real

Whatever the cause, shattered dreams require attention. If we minimize the pain, it will gradually destroy us like a cancer. Quite often, we don't need to have our dreams miraculously fulfilled, but we need to at least be convinced that God is in control and that he's teaching us a valuable lesson. That's one hard thing to do!

Can you relate to the lament of Psalm 42? When has your soul been downcast? Did you pour out your heart to God about it, like David did?

Describe the two types of shattered dreams. How do most people respond to each kind?

Reread Proverbs 13:12. Describe a time when your heart was sick because your hopes didn't come true. Did anyone help you through that time? Did you let anyone help you? If so, how?

Take a moment to read each one of these verses and think about how they apply to your life. Wherever you can do it, insert your name in the verses. Pray these passages over your heart.

- "Show me your ways, Lord, teach me your paths. Guide me in your truth and teach me, for you are God my Savior, and my hope is in you all day long" (Psalm 25:4-5).

- "May the God of hope fill you with all joy and peace as you trust in him, so that you may overflow with hope by the power of the Holy Spirit" (Romans 15:13).

- "Truly my soul finds rest in God; my salvation comes from him. Truly he is my rock and my salvation; he is my fortress, I will never be shaken" (Psalm 62:1-2).

Heart to Heart

How do we live out hope—practically and not just as an idea? Vaclav Havel, playwright and former President of Czechoslovakia, wisely observed:

> Hope is...not the conviction that something will turn out well, but the certainty that something makes sense, regardless of how it turns out.[1]

In this case, our greatest longing is for God's wisdom and perspective about our situations, and that's enough to fill our hearts again with hope. The challenge for me is to believe...and actually live like God really is enough.

~

God, I hate it when my world falls apart. Give me hope today through the promises of your Word. Even when it seems like my dreams are all shattered, I know that you are my constant. I want to put my hope in you, not my own dreams or accomplishments.

Day 4

Purified by Hope

*If we find ourselves with a desire that nothing in this
world can satisfy, the most probable explanation
is that we were made for another world.*

C.S. LEWIS

Are you empty? Exhausted? Yearning for something more? As women, we should be. Because we were never made to live in this fallen world. We were made for Eden, and for communion with God.

C.S. Lewis put it this way: "We are half-hearted creatures, fooling about with drink and sex and ambition when infinite joy is offered us, like an ignorant child who wants to go on making mud pies in a slum because he cannot imagine what is meant by the offer of a holiday at the sea. We are far too easily pleased."[1]

In this life as believers, we live squarely between the "already" and the "not yet." We've experienced God's wonderful grace to forgive us. He has made us his own dear children, and he has given us more meaning and purpose than we ever dreamed possible, but this is only a taste of what is to come.

In the Word

Read 1 John 3 today and pay special attention to verses 2-3:

Dear friends, now we are children of God, and what we will be has not yet been made known. But we know that when Christ appears, we shall be like him, for we shall see him as he is. All who have this hope in him purify themselves, just as he is pure.

Paul told the Christians in Ephesus that the Holy Spirit's presence and power in our lives is a "down payment" for all we'll enjoy when we see Jesus face-to-face. As wonderful as it is now to soak in God's love, our experience today doesn't hold a candle to the transformation and pure joy we'll find in the presence of God.

God has put it in all our hearts to long for heaven. Today, though, we have to live in the tension between what is and what will be. C.S. Lewis understood this tension, and he encourages us: "The settled happiness and security which we all desire, God withholds from us by the very nature of the world: but joy, pleasure, and merriment He has scattered broadcast…Our Father refreshes us on the journey with some pleasant inns, but will not encourage us to mistake them for home."[2]

In John's first letter, he points to the tension between our current spiritual state and the one to come, and he offers the contrast as a motivation to devote ourselves completely to God. If we really understand where we're going, John intimates, we won't let anything hinder us from running the race God has given us to run.

The writer to the Hebrews says those things come in two categories: sins and encumbrances. Both of these are like trying to carry a heavy backpack when we're running a race. It's counterproductive, and it just doesn't make sense. Focusing on the future reminds us what's most important today. When we realize that much of what the world values will someday burn up when everything passes through the fires of judgment, our thinking crystallizes and our choices become clearer.

Make It Real

Is it possible to focus too much on the glories we'll enjoy when we're with Jesus? Yes, I suppose so, but in our modern Christian culture, we focus far too much on the pleasures we want to enjoy today. John reminds us that a clear grasp of the future makes a difference in how we live today.

When we enjoy blessings and comforts, we don't take them for granted. We thank God and we share them with others. And when we suffer heartaches, we remember that there will come a day when every tear will be wiped away.

Blessings and adversity are simply tools in God's hands to remind us of his love and his purposes. When we grasp this fact, we won't feel guilty for enjoying the good things he gives us, and we won't sink into despair when things don't work out the way we hoped.

Do most people you know spend too much time thinking about the future when they'll see Jesus or pursuing pleasures today? What about you? What's the result of each focus?

Reread 1 John 3:2-3. What do you think it means that when we see Jesus we "shall be like him"?

How does focusing on hope for a glorious future with God purify your choices, motivations, and relationships today?

Take a moment to read each one of these verses and think about how they apply to your life. Wherever you can do it, insert your name in the verses. Pray these passages over your heart.

- "Do not let your hearts be troubled. You believe in God; believe also in me. My Father's house has many rooms; if that were not so, would I have told you that I am going there to prepare a place for you? And if I go and prepare a place for you, I will come back and take you to be with me that you also may be where I am" (John 14:1-3).

- "Therefore we do not lose heart. Though outwardly we are wasting away, yet inwardly we are being renewed day by day. For our light and momentary troubles are achieving for us an eternal glory that far outweighs them all. So we fix our eyes not on what is seen, but on what is unseen, since what is seen is temporary, but what is unseen is eternal" (2 Corinthians 4:16-18).

- "What no eye has seen, what no ear has heard, and what no human mind has conceived—the things God has prepared for those who love him" (1 Corinthians 2:9).

Heart to Heart

If we have hope in God's future for us, the difficulties we endure will take on new meaning. In his outstanding book *The Wounded Healer*, Henri Nouwen wrote:

> When we become aware that we do not have to escape our pains, but that we can mobilize them into a common search for life, those very pains are transformed from expressions of despair into signs of hope.[3]

Think often and deeply about what it will be like to be with Jesus, without the clouds of sin, doubt, and fear to prevent us from fully enjoying his love for us. Let this hope make a difference in how you live—in your choices about money and possessions, forgiving instead of holding grudges, and devoting your time to things that really matter.

⌒

God, my heart aches for home. Help me to live in this moment with eternity in view. To live in that blessed hope of one day being in your arms.

Day 5

Even When We Falter

Do not look to your hope, but to Christ,
the source of your hope.

CHARLES SPURGEON

What would it be like to fly? As a little girl, I would always wonder. Not in a jumbo jet, but like a bird—free from the cares and worries that weigh us down. David said the same thing: "Oh, that I had the wings of a dove! I would fly away and be at rest" (Psalm 55:6).

Hoping in God gives us wings, even when we falter. Even when we're tired. Weary. When we stumble and fall. Hope holds us up. It's the wind that propels us along, enabling us to not just survive, but to soar. Who wouldn't say "yes" to that?

In the Word

Read Isaiah 40 today and pay special attention to verses 30-31:

> *Even youths grow tired and weary, and young men stumble and fall; but those who hope in the LORD will renew their strength. They will soar on wings like eagles; they will run and not grow weary, they will walk and not be faint.*

Most of us can quote at least part of this beautiful verse in Isaiah about "soaring on wings like eagles," but we need to understand the context of this inspiring image. The people of God were anything but hopeful. They were deeply discouraged because they couldn't see God's hand at work in anything around them. In fact, they were so upset that they accused God of apathy: "You don't even care enough to notice our problems!"

Have you been there? I have. Sooner or later, all of us who walk with God feel that our prayers aren't making it past the ceiling. We feel alone, abandoned, and hopeless. In those times, it seems that God may be at work in everyone else's life, but he's forgotten all about us. Extraordinary hope is often born in times of gut-wrenching honesty when we can only muster the courage to complain to God that what he's doing (or not doing) doesn't seem fair. That's not much faith, but it's enough for God to work with.

When the people questioned the goodness of God, Isaiah reminded them of truth—not that God would instantly make their lives pleasant, but the fact that God is majestic in his power and attentive in his love. The prophet wrote in Isaiah 40:28-29:

> Do you not know? Have you not heard?
> The LORD is the everlasting God,
> the Creator of the ends of the earth.
> He will not grow tired or weary,
> and his understanding no one can fathom.
> He gives strength to the weary and increases
> the power of the weak.

No matter how bleak our situation may seem, Isaiah encourages us to keep trusting in God's goodness and greatness. No matter how long God takes to accomplish his purposes, the prophet tells us to cling to hope. If we look only at what we can see with our physical eyes, we'll quickly be discouraged. But if we have the eyes of faith and keep hoping in the one who works behind the scenes in the unseen world, our hearts can soar on wings like eagles even when we don't yet see God's hand at work.

Make It Real

Mary Lou Redding is an author, artist, and editor of *The Upper Room*. In her struggle to find hope in bleak circumstances, she learned to keep clinging to God. She writes:

> Our hope in God pulls us into the future. Hope allows
> us to affirm the reality of the abundant life that is ours in

Christ. Hope allows us to stand with those in pain and to hold them until they are able to feel the love of God for themselves again. Hope allows us to work to bring God's reign upon the earth even when we see no results. Our hope begins and ends in God, the source of all hope.[1]

Has there ever been a time when you felt God had abandoned you? What was that like for you?

Read over Isaiah 40:27-31 again. According to Isaiah, where does hope come from? How do we get it?

How might focusing on the goodness and greatness of God encourage you to keep hoping today?

Take a moment to read each one of these verses and think about how they apply to your life. Wherever you can do it, insert your name in the verses. Pray these passages over your heart.

- "I pray that the eyes of your heart may be enlightened in order that you may know the hope to which he has called you, the riches of his glorious inheritance in his holy people, and his incomparably great power for us who believe" (Ephesians 1:18-19).

- "We wait eagerly for our adoption to sonship, the redemption of our bodies. For in this hope we were saved. But hope that is seen is no hope at all. Who hopes for what they already have? But if we hope for what we do not yet have, we wait for it patiently" (Romans 8:23-25).

- "Let us draw near to God with a sincere heart and with the full assurance that faith brings, having our hearts sprinkled to cleanse us from a guilty conscience and having our bodies washed with pure water. Let us hold unswervingly to the hope we profess, for he who promised is faithful" (Hebrews 10:22-23).

Heart to Heart

Hope. Sometimes, it's tough to cling to. As Christians, our hope is far more than just a reassuring, happy feeling. R.C. Sproul describes it this way:

> Hope is called the anchor of the soul (Hebrews 6:19), because it gives stability to the Christian life. But hope is not simply a "wish" (I wish that such-and-such would take place); rather, it is that which latches on to the certainty of the promises of the future that God has made.[2]

How can you and I hold on to hope? *By holding on to Jesus.* We can't put our hope in our abilities to figure things out, or in our plan of how we insist God should work.

The only reality in this life that will never change is our relationship with Christ. "No one will snatch them out of my hand," Jesus said. He was talking about us, his daughters. We are safe and secure in our heavenly Father's grasp. Today, you and I can soar on the wings of God's promises and learn to fly, free of our worries and fears...no matter what life brings.

That's extraordinary hope!

⌒

Lord, so often I forget who you really are. Thank you for reminding me today of how good and powerful and loving you are. Renew my strength as I learn to hope in you, and when my strength runs out, carry me along with your strength. Give me wings to fly.

Extraordinary Beauty:
Radiance from an Authentic Heart

*[beauty:] all the aspects of a person
that are good, lovely, and attractive*

Chosen. Valued. Desired. We all long to be thought of as beautiful, but too often, we look in the mirror or examine our hearts and become disappointed—very disappointed—with ourselves. Are you tired of the fashion model hype? Ready to rediscover true beauty? This week, we'll try to see ourselves through God's eyes and glimpse at the intrinsic beauty in all of us.

Eve certainly got the response we all hope for when Adam saw her in all her glory for the first time! And Lydia learned to enjoy beautiful things as gifts from God. They weren't obsessions, and they weren't distractions. We will learn a lot from these two women.

We'll also look at other insights about beauty that will inspire us, comfort us, and point us toward God so that we delight in his beauty.

Day 1

Satisfied

Heat cannot be separated from fire,
or beauty from the Eternal.

DANTE ALIGHIERI

Our beauty isn't just external. God created us to be beautiful internally as well. And when our hearts are full of his love and grace, we act beautifully in all we do. Eve was confident in her beauty without letting it go to her head. She wasn't proud or haughty. She didn't degrade or devalue herself. On the contrary, Eve was *unashamed* in her beauty.

In the Word

Read Genesis 2 today and pay special attention to verses 23-25:

> *The man said, "This is now bone of my bones and flesh of my flesh; she shall be called 'woman,' for she was taken out of man." That is why a man leaves his father and mother and is united to his wife, and they become one flesh. Adam and his wife were both naked, and they felt no shame.*

On the day Eve was created and presented to Adam, his eyes were captivated by her beauty. His comment could be translated, "Wow! Look at her!" He was thrilled with Eve, and in the safety and security of their relationship, they were naked and unashamed.

Is physical beauty worthless? No. How could it be? God created it! Many women in Christian circles degrade and devalue themselves, thinking that physical beauty is evil or, at best, worthless. This is simply not true. Look around at creation—the evidence abounds for God's appreciation of and knack for beauty! If we call beauty all the aspects of a person that are good, lovely, and attractive, God is the epitome of beauty.

It follows, then, that everything God creates is beautiful, because God has called it "good." Go back and look over the creation account in Genesis 1. God describes all he has made as "good"…six different times. And human beings? God said more. He called them "very good." You and I have been created in God's image, so how can we not bear the mark of his beauty?

In a beautiful psalm, King David reminds us that our appearance is no accident. He wrote, "I praise you because I am fearfully and wonderfully made; your works are wonderful, I know that full well" (Psalm 139:14). We often neglect our appearance or become obsessed with it, forgetting that God had a gracious hand in creating each of us exactly the way we are.

How would you have felt if you had been Eve that day when your husband was so thrilled to see you in your naked glory?

Make It Real

Everywhere we look we see images of gorgeous young women who are endowed with effortless beauty. The not-so-subtle message is that if we don't look like them all day, every day, we're second-class women. And this perception hurts our hearts.

Comparison kills in every area of life—our children, our careers, our finances, our vacations, our cars, our houses, and on and on—but comparing our appearance may be the most devastating to our sense of joy and peace. We all tend to compare ourselves to the women around us and, more damaging, to the airbrushed images of women around us. From cover images on magazines to billboard advertisements, we are exposed to an unreal version of beauty. And no woman in real life can or should compete with today's models and computer-modified images.

It may be small consolation, but the gorgeous models we long to look like often don't feel deep satisfaction either. Many suffer with anxiety and depression and try to ease their fears with drugs, alcohol, and self-deprivation. Even for them, the comparison game produces a sense of loss. That's because we are never satisfied when we base our worth on others. God didn't create us to play the comparison game. We are created in God's image, and as women, we uniquely express the beauty, tenderness, and compassion of God.

Eve "felt no shame." Shame shows itself in extremes of behavior. We often think of shame crushing people's spirits and causing them to withdraw to hide from others. But many women respond to their shame in the opposite way. They feel compelled to prove their value by being the smartest, wittiest, and prettiest girl around. Shame robs us of true contentment, keeps us from being real, and leaves us longing for more...always more.

> How does shame show up in your life? Do you feel driven to give up your beauty? How are you compelled to prove your beauty? Be honest.

> All of us struggle with a degree of insecurity. What areas do *you* feel most insecure about?

> Read Psalm 139:13-17. How can understanding that you are "fearfully and wonderfully made" help you experience true satisfaction instead of comparing yourself with others?

Take a moment to read each one of these verses and think about how they apply to your life. Wherever you can do it, insert your name in the verses. Pray these passages over your heart.

- "He has made everything beautiful in his time" (Ecclesiastes 3:11).

- "You are altogether beautiful, my darling; there is no flaw in you" (Song of Solomon 4:7).

- "Charm is deceptive, and beauty is fleeting, but a woman who fears the LORD is to be praised" (Proverbs 31:30).

Heart to Heart

You may have natural beauty, but I don't. It takes a little while to get dressed and out the door in the morning! My daughter Megan has natural physical beauty, but I promise you that what really makes her beautiful is her heart—the inside.

I admit that I love wearing Mac makeup, stylish heels, and a nice dress to feel like a princess for a day. (After all, if the barn needs painting, paint it!) But for God's woman, this physical beauty is a shadow of her loving, tender, considerate heart. Humility. Joy. Compassion. Humor. Love. Faith. That's her beauty.

American author Anne Roiphe wisely wrote, "A woman whose smile is open and whose expression is glad has a kind of beauty no matter what she wears."[1] This kind of beauty grows with time, rather than diminishing. Wrinkles can't even stop it! Nor can menopause, cancer, or any type of hardship. It's the imperishable quality of a gentle and quiet spirit which is precious in the sight of God.

⌒

Lord, I praise you because you have made me just exactly the way you wanted me. Help me to get free to receive and express that beauty in me. God, free me from the shame, insecurity, and even anger I feel sometimes about myself. Show me how precious and beautiful I am to you.

Day 2

Enjoy Beauty

Beauty without virtue is a flower without perfume.
FRENCH PROVERB

If God created beauty, he made it to be enjoyed. We can be women of extremes, can't we? Some of us are so caught up in looking great that we seldom give a thought to God's purposes for beauty. Others are so repulsed by all the glitz and glamour that we pursue plainness with a passion! Lydia was a woman who found the right balance.

In the Word

Read Acts 16:11-15 today and pay special attention to verses 14-15:

> *One of those listening was a woman named Lydia, a dealer in purple cloth from the city of Thyatira, who was a worshiper of God. The Lord opened her heart to respond to Paul's message. When she and the members of her household were baptized, she invited us to her home.*

Lydia worked in the fashion world. She was a businesswoman who sold highly-prized purple cloth. In those days, purple dye was rare and expensive, so oftentimes, only royalty could afford it. Scholars say that an ounce of purple dye likely cost more than a pound of gold!

The apostle Paul met Lydia by the river outside the city of Philippi, and he told her about Jesus. God opened Lydia's heart, and she responded to the message of Christ's forgiveness.

What did Lydia do immediately after becoming a Christian? Circle the correct answer.

1. Quit her job in the fashion world

2. Burned her purple cloth

3. Invited Paul and Silas over

4. Became a nun

This woman opened up her home to Paul and Silas, providing them a place to stay while they were in the city. As a merchant, it's likely that Lydia had a large home, with plenty of room for guests. By welcoming these strangers in, Lydia showed that she was putting her faith into action.

Lydia didn't need to repent of being a merchant or of valuing fine fabrics, and she didn't have to be ashamed for enjoying the beautiful things in life. But here's the key: Lydia used what she had—the resources God had blessed her with—to encourage, bless, and support other people. As a Christian, Lydia's life wasn't all about *her* anymore.

Lydia's example suggests that we can (and should!) enjoy beauty. Fashion, clothing design, and style are examples of how God has made this world to be beautiful, not just functional. Are there extremes? Of course! We go wrong when we allow beauty to become our sole focus. In Ezekiel 16:10-12, God uses the imagery of beautiful clothing to describe his care for his people:

> I clothed you with an embroidered dress and put sandals of fine leather on you. I dressed you in fine linen and covered you with costly garments. I adorned you with jewelry: I put bracelets on your arms and a necklace around your neck, and I put a ring on your nose, earrings on your ears and a beautiful crown on your head.

Wow. Talk about beautiful! Go back and circle every item mentioned that relates to fashion. Bracelets, necklaces, rings…the whole shebang! It seems pretty obvious that God himself enjoys beauty. But beauty out of balance can be dangerous.

But after that passage comes a rebuke to Israel (and to us): "But you trusted in your beauty and used your fame to become a prostitute" (Ezekiel 16:15). Hard words. God calls his people out not for being beautiful, but for trusting in their beauty rather than in God. More than just literal prostitution, God is speaking of anytime you or I use our beauty to bring glory to ourselves, rather than God. When we do this, we worship and serve created things, rather than our Creator.

Make It Real

You can be beautiful without being provocative. There, I said it. Do you really believe that? Many of us lean toward one extreme in how we respond to beauty. Which category sounds like you?

- *Joyless legalism*: We cut ourselves down and neglect our appearance, thinking that the *only* thing God cares about is our hearts. We somehow think that looking pretty is wrong or sinful (think of all the letters of encouragement we could write while *other* women are putting on their makeup!) Sadly, we fail to express the image of God in our beauty.

- *Self-serving vanity*: We are obsessed with how we look and find our security in our physical attractiveness. We *have* to have the perfect nails, every hair in place, and the latest trend in dress. We feel pressure to be "put together," but we neglect our hearts. We often judge other people based on their looks rather than showing compassion.

Have you seen women out of balance about beauty, some pursuing it at all costs and some who have given up on it?

I'm guessing you're not a dealer of purple cloth; yet, Lydia offers a great example of how to care for yourself—to find your beauty and creativity.

Do you allow yourself to enjoy beauty? Have you made beauty an idol? What would a balanced approach look like for you?

Take a moment to read each one of these verses and think about how they apply to your life. Wherever you can do it, insert your name in the verses. Pray these passages over your heart.

- "You are precious and honored in my sight, and…I love you" (Isaiah 43:4).
- "You are a chosen people, a royal priesthood, a holy nation, God's special possession" (1 Peter 2:9).
- "Do nothing out of selfish ambition or vain conceit. Rather, in humility consider others above yourselves" (Philippians 2:3).

Heart to Heart

It's very satisfying to find the perfect outfit…especially on sale. However, satisfaction quickly fades when that game of comparison sneaks up on us. At a friend's recent birthday party, I noticed a woman across the room wearing *my* dress, only a few sizes smaller. Talk about intimidating! My mind was already sizing her up, comparing how we both looked.

Wait a minute, Julie, I thought. *Who's the woman behind the dress? Is she beautiful?* We've all been there before. Maybe it wasn't a dress or a party, but I know you've caught yourself comparing your body, your hair, and your outfit with another woman's.

Who are you behind your dress? Sure, take a look in your closet, but also take a look in your heart. Have you been neglecting the only kind of beauty that really lasts? Your beauty isn't just a matter of what you wear, but who you are.

⌐

God, thank you for everything you are teaching me about beauty. Convict my heart and show me how to honor you in the way I dress, act, and carry myself. Open my eyes to how I can creatively pursue and express my beauty.

Day 3

Revealed

The fountain of beauty is the heart.

FRANCIS QUARLES

uthor Stasi Eldredge asks an important and revealing question:
"What if you have a genuine and captivating beauty that is marred
only by your striving?"[1] First Peter 3 challenges us that as we put on
our makeup and get ready in the morning, we must also remember to
beautify our hearts.

In the Word

Read 1 Peter 3:1-8 today and pay special attention to verses 3-4:

> *Your beauty should not come from outward adornment, such
> as elaborate hairstyles and the wearing of gold jewelry or fine
> clothes. Rather, it should be that of your inner self, the unfad-
> ing beauty of a gentle and quiet spirit, which is of great worth
> in God's sight.*

Things haven't changed much in two thousand years, have they?
When Peter wrote this letter to early Christians, women were tempted
to value their appearance more than their hearts. If Peter looked at a
magazine rack today, he'd probably shake his head and wonder if anybody had paid attention to his letter all these years.

Let's take a look at what Peter's really saying. Go back over verses 3-4
and fill in the blanks to discover the characteristics of beauty:

Inner Beauty:

• _____

• _____

• _____

Outer Beauty:

• _____

• _____

• _____

Peter reminds us that inner beauty is unfading. Imperishable. It can't be destroyed. It gets more beautiful with time. It doesn't sag, and it doesn't quit working when we get a little older. What's real beauty to God? Peter describes it as a "gentle and quiet spirit." I don't think God is asking us to take vows of silence. He's talking about something more. Let's take a closer look:

• *Gentle* means *exercising God's strength under his control.*

• *Quiet* means *steady and settled due to a divinely-inspired inner calmness.*

Is this different from what you thought? As women, we develop gentle and quiet spirits by being with Jesus, the one who describes himself as "gentle and humble in heart."

Make It Real

Ever met her? She's big on appearances, with Bible in hand. She is ever-learning but never coming to the knowledge of the truth. But what you see on the outside ain't what's on the inside. The Word has never gone from her head to her heart. And so, she is not changed by it. Ouch! I've seen glimpses of this attitude in myself at times.

The inner beauty of gentle and quiet women is revealed in reverent behavior, encouragement, a love for others (especially our husband and children), sensibility, purity, kindness, diligence, and honoring God's Word. When we value what God values, it makes him smile. Let's be women who are bold in our fervor for the Lord, but are also gentle and quiet in our spirit.

What misconceptions have you had about a "gentle and quiet spirit" and inner beauty?

Who is someone you know who is a terrific example of a strong woman with a gentle and quiet spirit? What is it in her that reveals her inner beauty?

Read 1 Peter 3:3-5 again. How much attention and resources should we devote to our bodies? Our hearts? How can you move toward a balance?

Take a moment to read each one of these verses and think about how they apply to your life. Wherever you can do it, insert your name in the verses. Pray these passages over your heart.

- "Therefore, as God's chosen people, holy and dearly loved, clothe yourselves with compassion, kindness, humility, gentleness and patience" (Colossians 3:12).

- "Whatever is true, whatever is noble, whatever is right, whatever is pure, whatever is lovely, whatever is admirable...think about such things" (Philippians 4:8).

Heart to Heart

At the core of it, beauty is a heart issue. It's so freeing for me to realize that I don't have to frequent the spa or get plastic surgery in order to be beautiful to God. Like 1 Samuel 16:7 says, "The LORD looks at the heart."

If beauty includes all the aspects of a woman that are good, lovely, and attractive, then unfading beauty is found in my heart when I am genuine and caring. And having a heart like that doesn't just happen. It's a journey. A lifetime of allowing God to shape and mold our hearts.

Lord, I bring to you my heart, even the ugly parts. Grow in me and reveal to me true, inner beauty. Ground me in the truths of who you are. Heal the wounds I carry around. Give me your love for other people.

Day 4

Sensual Beauty

God made every one of us a sexual being, and
that is good. Attraction and arousal are the natural,
spontaneous, God-given responses to physical beauty.

RICK WARREN

Go d created sex for physical pleasure between a husband and wife. In the context of marriage, sexual intimacy is good. Beautiful. God-honoring. Holy. In fact, it's worship. While many Christians view sex as bad or dirty, a woman of godly beauty delights and rejoices in her sexuality as a God-given gift to be shared with her man. It's time to redeem our sexuality.

In the Word

Read Song of Solomon 7 today and pay special attention to verses 6-8:

> *"How beautiful you are and how pleasing, my love, with your delights! Your stature is like that of the palm, and your breasts like clusters of fruit. I said, 'I will climb the palm tree; I will take hold of its fruit.'"*

For centuries, Bible scholars didn't know what to make of the little book in the Bible called Song of Solomon. It describes a beautiful, sensual love between a man and his bride, but the vast majority of scholars couldn't handle it. They labeled it an allegory of Christ and the church, or an illustration of Israel's relationship with God. Perhaps it is.

But Song of Solomon is also a highly sensuous poem of passionate affection. In chapter 7, Solomon takes great care to describe in detail the beauty of his bride's body, from her sandaled feet to her flowing locks of hair…and everything in between. Starting with verse 1, take a moment to write these descriptions out:

Example: Legs like *jewels*

- A navel like _____
- A waist like _____
- Breasts like _____
- A neck like _____
- Eyes like _____
- A nose like _____
- A head like _____
- Hair like _____

Some of these terms may be a bit confusing because they contain Jewish cultural references, but one thing is obvious: Solomon treasured his bride. He delighted in every intricate detail of her sensuous beauty! And his beloved was delighted to give herself to him. Wholly. Completely. Without shame. "I belong to my beloved," she exclaims, "and his desire is for me."

As I read this passage, I am awestruck by the beauty of unfettered intimacy. There's not a hint of guilt or shame in this couple's words. No embarrassment. No hesitation. No fear. Just pure delight in the beauty God has created in each other's bodies.

Sex is a gift of God to be enjoyed by a husband and a wife with complete freedom, creativity, and pleasure. Far from being dirty or shameful, sex was God's idea in the first place! In marriage, the joy of sex enables the couple to "become one flesh"—one in heart, mind, and body. Far too often, however, Christians settle for something less—far less—than the pure beauty of God's design for their sexuality.

Make It Real

In a culture that devalues the mystery and beauty of sexual intimacy, Solomon reminds us of the freedom and joy of sex as God intended.

Today's study isn't just about the physical, biological act. God created you as a uniquely sexual being. Your sexuality is precious to Him…not dirty, evil, or unimportant. Understanding our sexuality biblically is critical.

All of us have a slightly different view of sex, based on our family, experiences, and culture. Maybe you've experienced sexual abuse of some kind and wonder if you'll ever be able to actually enjoy sex. Maybe you've engaged in sexual experiences outside of marriage and struggle with guilt. Maybe you are sexually pure, but are hesitant about actually *enjoying* sex because you tend to view it as dirty or wrong… something to be endured.

Our God is a God of healing, hope, and redemption. Whatever your sexual experiences in the past, and whatever you feel today as a result, I want you to know that God longs to restore the sanctity of your sexuality and give you beauty for ashes. In the context of marriage, God longs for you to fully enjoy the beauty of sex without inhibition, doubt, fear, or regret.

Great sex begins long before the couple enters the bedroom. Treating each other with affection and respect during the day is the foreplay you and your husband need to be relaxed and excited about enjoying sex together.

What are some creative ways you can show him respect and affection throughout the day?

Read Proverbs 5:18-19. How would you feel if your husband delighted in you this way?

Read Hebrews 13:4. An undefiled marriage bed begins with an honorable marriage. How could you be more honoring in order to bring sexual freedom?

What would sex look like in your marriage with no inhibitions, doubts, fears, or regrets? Do you and your husband need to work on your communication, your experimentation, or your understanding of one another?

Take a moment to read each one of these verses and think about how they apply to your life. Wherever you can do it, insert your name in the verses. Pray these passages over your heart.

- "My beloved is mine and I am his; he browses among the lilies" (Song of Solomon 2:16).
- "Marriage should be honored by all, and the marriage bed kept pure" (Hebrews 13:4).
- "Let him kiss me with the kisses of his mouth—for your love is more delightful than wine. Take me away...Let the king bring me into his chambers" (Song of Solomon 1:2,4).

Heart to Heart

Like many women, I struggle with self-esteem. Sometimes I actually pay attention when Satan whispers the lies that I am ugly, plain, or no good. This is simply not true! We are beautiful and valued in God's eyes and he wants us to delight in our sexuality.

If you are married, I encourage you to talk to your husband about your desires, hopes, and fears about sexual intimacy, even if it feels awkward at first. Don't be afraid of disappointing him by bringing it up. He has probably been wondering how to build the courage to start the same conversation. Vulnerability is scary. But communication allows our fears to be replaced with tenderness and understanding.

Some of us have had traumatic sexual experiences in the past, so we shut down when we try to talk about or engage in sexual activity. Some of us are ashamed of our bodies or our performance. Some of us don't fully understand how God created the female body to experience sexual pleasure.

But the pressure's off! Don't be ashamed or embarrassed to explore the sensuous beauty of great sex with your husband. If you find yourself struggling, see your doctor or a professional Christian counselor. It is time to delight in God in this area of your life...God made sex for you and your husband to enjoy!

~

Lord, thank you for creating me as a woman and as a sexual being. Bring healing in my heart when and where I feel shame or pain. Free me to enjoy sexual intimacy in all of its beauty, just as you intended it to be.

Day 5

Finding God's Beauty

If you see any beauty in Christ, and say,
"I desire to have that," God will work it in you.

G.V. WIGRAM

God's beauty runs deep. We will never truly understand our beauty until we see and experience the beauty of God in all of his splendor. David knew that beholding God's beauty changes everything.

In the Word

Read Psalm 27 today and pay special attention to verse 4:

> *One thing I ask of the LORD, this only do I seek: that I may dwell in the house of the LORD all the days of my life, to gaze upon the beauty of the LORD and to seek him in his temple.*

If Satan can't make you bad, he will make you busy. Being busy in the "good" things often robs us of the "best" things. Busy has wisely been defined as **B**eing **U**nder **S**atan's **Y**oke. Revisit your focus verse with that in mind. What was the most important thing to David?

_____

Crazy, huh? *One thing.* David didn't ask God for ten things or five things. King David didn't even have a top two selection. No matter how much pressure he felt, he disciplined his heart to "gaze upon the beauty of the LORD and to seek him in his temple." David could have just said, "I'll go to church on Sunday...and Wednesday I'll go to Bible study and small group...and then I'll be close to God." But he didn't. Let's look at verse 4 again. What are the key verbs?

- _____
- _____
- _____
- _____

David wasn't just rattling off a list of "quiet time" key words. This man wanted to experience God. He would not settle for a stale, obligatory relationship with God or going-through-the-motions spirituality. Notice that the words you wrote above are primarily all about *focus*. Not a checklist of certain "Christian behaviors." David wanted to "gaze upon the beauty of the LORD." Is God beautiful to you and me today? If not, what are we missing? After all, the beautiful God that David describes has not changed. Perhaps we're distracted. Perhaps we're worshipping our own idea of God. As psychologist, author, and Bible teacher Larry Crabb points out, many of us tend to see God as an "especially attentive waiter."[1] If God gives us good service, we give him a nice tip of praise or money. But if he doesn't do what we want him to do, we complain and look somewhere else for service.

This kind of perspective about God seldom lets us see his beauty. We're so consumed with our stuff, our junk, our trials—the day-to-day responsibilities that clamor for our attention—that we begin to believe God exists for us, to make us happy. And when God doesn't respond the way we think he should, we grow angry, bitter, and jaded. What about you? Was there a time recently when you viewed God as your "waiter"?

Make It Real

One of my favorite moments in C. S. Lewis' Chronicles of Narnia is in the book *The Lion, the Witch, and the Wardrobe*. Mrs. Beaver tells Lucy about Aslan, the elusive lion of Narnia, who is a symbol of Christ in Lewis' stories. As Mrs. Beaver talks about Aslan's power and majesty, Lucy feels overwhelmed with the thought that she might someday actually face the awesome beast. Lucy is afraid. She timidly asks if Aslan is safe.

Mr. Beaver shakes his head. "'Course he isn't safe," he says. "But he's good."[2] *He's good.* Jesus is magnificent and beautiful beyond description. Awesome and tender. Majestic and kind. He leads us through valleys and up to mountains. And sometimes, in the darkness, we can't see him. Like Lucy, we may be timid because we aren't sure if he's safe, but we can cling to him because we're sure that he is, indeed, good.

Check out verse 5: "For in the day of trouble he will keep me safe in his dwelling; he will hide me in the shelter of his sacred tent and set me high upon a rock." This is why God is beautiful to David. Because he is good. Faithful. Strong. Kind. As we see God for who he is, we are moved to offer up sacrifices of worship…not just with our lips, but with our lives.

Do you see God today? Is anything preventing you from gazing upon the beauty of the Lord?

What do the words you speak each day say about your view of God's greatness and goodness?

God is jealous for you, his daughter, to know and experience him. Gaze on his beauty. Not just out of duty, but out of desire. Ask him today to clear the eyes of your heart to see him.

Take a moment to read each one of these verses and think about how they apply to your life. Wherever you can do it, insert your name in the verses. Pray these passages over your heart.

- "You make known to me the path of life; you will fill me with joy in your presence, with eternal pleasures at your right hand" (Psalm 16:11).

- "Worship the LORD in the splendour of his holiness" (Psalm 29:2).

- "Who among the gods is like you, Lord? Who is like you—majestic in holiness, awesome in glory, working wonders?" (Exodus 15:11).

Heart to Heart

How do we know what we really believe about God? Jesus said that our words reflect our heart's true condition: "For the mouth speaks what the heart is full of" (Matthew 12:34). Stop and think:

- When times are good, what words flow from my mouth to those around me and to God?
- When I'm stressed, what words overflow from my heart?

The more that you and I *ask, seek, dwell,* and *gaze,* the more we will see God for who he is. And if God is beautiful as David describes him, he deserves all our attention. Maybe that's why God made it so clear: "You shall have no other gods before me" (Exodus 20:3). God is awesome in his power and gentle in his kindness. The more we grapple with these ideas, the more we can trust him with the ups and downs we experience each day.

⌒

Lord, so often, I misunderstand who you are. Open my eyes today to see you. Show me your beauty, goodness, holiness, and love…and grow your beauty in me.

Extraordinary Healing:
When Life Hurts

*[healing:] the gut-wrenching journey through brokenness
toward restoration, wholeness, and a fully alive heart*

A few of us enjoy charmed lives for a while. But sooner or later, every woman experiences the devastation of suffering and loss. We face death, disease, wayward children, and heartaches of every description. Most of us try to run from our pain. We try to cope. But deep inside, we wonder if life will ever be "normal" again.

I believe there are two types of people: those who have been shattered by loss and never recovered, and those who have found the heart and courage to learn life's deepest lessons in the darkness they've faced.

This week, we'll look at the stories of Rachel and the woman who reached out to touch Jesus. Both of these women experienced deep pain, but found true healing in God. Real healing isn't just relief from the suffering; it's an open door to see God (and ourselves) in a brand new way—to see a new world of insights, wisdom, contentment, and connection with other people and God.

watch for the "as it turned outs" in Scripture

Day 1

How Long?

*Jesus willingly chose isolation so you might
never be alone in your hurt and sorrow.*
JONI EARECKSON TADA

Jacob waltzed into Rachel's life just like in a fairy tale, but not for long. Life served up one disappointment after the next: On Rachel's wedding day, her sister Leah got the man. When she finally did get married, she couldn't have kids, and Leah rubbed it in. Last ditch effort? Her brilliant idea of a "quick fix" utterly failed. And that's when God stepped in...

In the Word

Read Genesis 30:1-24 this week and pay special attention to verse 1:

> *When Rachel saw that she was not bearing Jacob any children,
> she became jealous of her sister. So she said to Jacob, "Give me
> children, or I'll die!"*

Jacob rode into town on a beautiful horse (okay, probably not, but I'm trying to create a romantic picture) as a young, handsome stranger. Soon, he had his eye on Rachel, and he made her father Laban an offer he couldn't refuse—to work seven years for her hand.

Every woman has nightmares of wedding bloopers. But I guarantee, Rachel's was worse than anything you can imagine. Her father tricked the couple by giving Rachel's older sister Leah to the unsuspecting Jacob on the wedding night. To win the girl of his dreams, Jacob agreed to work another seven years. (Talk about love!)

As you can imagine, the marriage triangle didn't work very well. In Jewish culture, having sons was considered a sign of God's blessing. Leah gave Jacob son after son, but Rachel was barren. She endured the pain of seeing her sister bask in delight (and a fair share of gloating) as she fed and played with her beloved sons, year after year. Eventually the shame, ridicule, hurt, and anger exploded. Rachel lost it. Look at your focus verse to see what she said when she couldn't handle the pain and humiliation a moment longer.

We can assume that Jacob had been doing his fair share to create children, so Rachel's outburst was more toward God than her husband. She was hurt, frustrated, and no doubt angry at God. Just like many of us, Rachel was a fan of the "do it myself" approach. Rather than looking for God in the midst of her pain, she looked for a quick solution to the pain.

Enter Bilhah. In her impatience, Rachel, like Sarah years before, presented her maid to her husband and told him, "Sleep with her so that she can bear children for me and I too can build a family through her" (verse 3). Makes sense...only it wasn't what God wanted, and it led to a whole lot of chaos. Rachel's attempts to fix the whole kid situation utterly failed, leading to huge conflict and strife in the family (can you imagine conversation at the dinner table?).

The punch line of this fairy tale-gone-bad shows up in one little statement in verse 22, "Then God remembered Rachel; he listened to her."

Even when Rachel panicked, God did not forget his promise. He never does. Rachel finally conceived and had a son, Joseph. God listened to her. He listens to you, too.

Make It Real

When life gets crazy we'll do anything to feel better...to numb the pain. In our desperate search for a solution, we often make wrong choices such as:

- Obsess about *fixing the problem* in our own strength and wisdom (like Rachel).

- Become addicted to *doing,* living perfectionistic, put-together lives.
- Shut down our hearts, so we *don't feel* anything.
- Latch on to anyone/anything that makes us happy, so we end up *addicted* to an unhealthy relationship or situation.

Can you identify with any of these statements? Which ones?

Are you running from pain and brokenness in your life? Ignoring it? How are you trying to "fix it," like Rachel?

What are some reasons women may not want to be honest with God about their pain, disappointment, and heartache?

Read Psalm 13. How does David's perception of God and his situation change by the end of the psalm?

Pray and ask God for the courage to open your spirit and address the core of your brokenness and loss. Do you feel stuck? Alone? Depressed? Hopeless? Pour it all out to him.

Take a moment to read each one of these verses and think about how they apply to your life. Wherever you can, insert your name in the verses. Pray these passages over your heart.

- "I will restore you to health and heal your wounds" (Jeremiah 30:17).
- "Praise the LORD, my soul, and forget not all His benefits —who forgives all your sins and heals all your diseases" (Psalm 103:2-3).

Heart to Heart

I'll never forget the night Zach and I were driving home late after a game. *Bam!* We hit the poor deer head-on. Shattered glass lay all around us on the seats, and the hood was crumpled in a mass of tangled steel. We were pretty shaken, but safe.

A car can be fixed in a couple weeks. But the healing of wounded hearts requires a journey. Sometimes, God uses wrecked plans and shattered dreams to propel us into a deeper encounter with him. Read Psalm 34:18: "The Lord is close to the brokenhearted and saves those who are crushed in spirit." In Hebrew, *brokenhearted* means hurt. Demolished. Destroyed. Fractured. Injured. Shattered. Smashed. Torn down.

Your reasons might be different, but can you identify with the depth of Rachel's anger? Are you outraged because your father walked out on your family? Crushed because labs were positive for cancer? Maybe your spouse betrayed you? We all have our own version of "crazy."

The Bible says that the Lord is close to the brokenhearted. That God will never leave you or forsake you, and that your heavenly Father cries with you and holds your tears in a bottle. Your honesty with God opens your heart to receive his tenderness, wisdom, and comfort.

In Psalm 13, David was frustrated and hurt. Four times in the first two verses, he pleads, "How long, O Lord?" And he even asks, "Will you forget me forever?" God isn't shocked when we are honest with him about our pain, and he doesn't tell us, "Just get over it." He enters our pain with us and remains present in his love and strength even when everyone else walks away.

Don't deny your brokenness. And don't panic. Bring your heart to the only one who can bring healing. And rest in his love for you. The crazy thing is that when you and I are most broken, we get to know and experience God in ways we never imagined.

~

God, so often I have panicked and tried to solve things
on my own. I need you. Desperately. Comfort me and
show me that your promises are real, even to me.

Day 2

Don't Run Away

God will mend a broken heart if you give him all the pieces.

AESOP

Hiding and healing are not the same thing. You and I don't gain anything by denying our brokenness. We might like to resolve troubles immediately, but when it comes to our hearts, there are no quick fixes. We aren't equipped to instantly heal. Instantly move on. The woman in today's story learns that healing begins when we come out of hiding and start running to Jesus. Crying out to him. Being gut honest.

In the Word

Read Luke 8:40-48 today and pay special attention to verses 47-48:

> *Then the woman, seeing that she could not go unnoticed, came trembling and fell at his feet. In the presence of all the people, she told why she had touched him and how she had been instantly healed. Then he said to her, "Daughter, your faith has healed you. Go in peace."*

It's often been said that "desperate people do desperate things." This woman was desperate. She had been bleeding for 12 years, but the doctors couldn't find a cure. In that culture, she had become an outcast. Sickness was viewed as God's divine judgment for a misguided, sinful life.

To the people in her day, she had become less than nothing, but there was something special about her—she still had an ounce of hope.

She had heard of a Rabbi who could work miracles of healing, and he was her last, thin thread of hope for a cure. She heard that he was passing through her town, so she stationed herself in the growing crowd outside. Finally he came into view. He was going to walk right past her!

At that moment, the woman did something radical. Desperate, she bent down and reached through the legs of the people in front of her. With all the strength she had in her sick and frail body, she reached out for life. For healing. For Jesus. When she touched him, she was immediately healed!

Suddenly, her delight changed to panic. The man had stopped and was walking back toward her. The crowd parted, and he caught her eye. She felt terribly exposed, but something in his expression told her he was safe. She fell at his feet and told him the whole story "in the presence of all the people." The same people who had ostracized her all these years.

Jesus didn't try to rush her, even though he had been hurrying to the side of a dying girl. He patiently listened, smiled, and said tenderly, "Daughter, your faith has healed you. Go in peace."

Make It Real

Can you imagine hearing those words after 12 years of suffering? Here's the point: *Healing does not happen when we run away from our pain.* When we are hurting, all we want is relief—and we want it now! But God wants to use every moment to deepen our relationship with him. On that busy street, Jesus could have kept right on walking, but he didn't. His power had gone out to a hurting woman, and he wanted to connect and show his love for her.

God doesn't want a business relationship with us, his daughters. We are more than consumers of his grace products. He loves us deeply, and desires an intimate, loving relationship with us. One of my favorite word pictures of God's heart is in Isaiah's prediction of the Messiah: "A bruised reed he will not break, and a smoldering wick he will not snuff out. In faithfulness he will bring forth justice" (Isaiah 42:3). This insight changes how I respond to hurt and pain in my life. Instead of just wanting it over quickly, I believe God will show up and make himself real to me in the midst of it. Pain and disappointment can cause us to doubt God's goodness and love. But we can't judge God's faithfulness by our perception. We must trust that God is at work, even when we can't see him.

Revisit Luke 8:40-48. What do you think it meant to this woman for Jesus to stop and talk with her?

Why is it important to understand that God wants a relationship with us, not just to give us pain relief?

Run. We all do it. How have you been running from your pain and brokenness?

What would it look like for you to "reach out" to Jesus?

Take a moment to read each one of these verses and think about how they apply to your life. Wherever you can do it, insert your name in the verses. Pray these passages over your heart.

- "LORD my God, I called to you for help, and you healed me" (Psalm 30:2).

- "He heals the brokenhearted and binds up their wounds... Great is our Lord, and mighty in power" (Psalm 147:3,5).

- "Because of the LORD's great love we are not consumed, for his compassions never fail. They are new every morning; great is your faithfulness" (Lamentations 3:22-23).

Heart to Heart

I play "hide and seek" with God, sometimes. As much as I want to *know* God, when I'm hurting or afraid, I kind of prefer to hide. In my head, I know I should run to Jesus, the source of my life and hope, but sometimes, in the moment of strife, I just want to run away.

Disappointment. Frustration. Anguish. Failure. In moments like these, what do we do?

- *We choose to hide.* Behind our makeup. Behind our outfits. We say we're fine.

- *We choose to run away.* We think we can outrun our pain, and leave it in the past.

- *We choose to sit and do nothing.* We are enveloped by our pain, and we give up hope.

Many of us paste on smiles while covering up hearts that are dying. Why do we hide, run away, sit paralyzed? Several reasons, maybe. We're afraid of being exposed. Of getting hurt to a greater extent. We're desperately trying to stay in control and fix ourselves and our situations. We're prideful. Selfish. We don't want to expose our weakness.

Here's the amazing thing: God invites us to cry out to him. To run to him. To be completely, ruthlessly honest with him. About everything, whether it's conflict with our spouse, rebellious kids, stress at work, or any number of the daily realities that we women face.

"Come to me," Jesus invites us, "all you who are weary and burdened, and I will give you rest" (Matthew 11:28).

Jesus, I want to reach out and touch you. I need healing for my hurt, my pain. Speak to me like you did with the woman who reached out and touched you.

Day 3

When It Doesn't Make Sense

Snuggle in God's arms. When you are hurting, when you feel lonely, left out. Let Him cradle you, comfort you, reassure you of His all-sufficient power and love.

KAY ARTHUR

Life is all a matter of perspective. If you've ever gotten tumbled in the ocean waves, you know the feeling of being completely out of control. Try as you might, there's nothing you can do. Except hold your breath and wait for the inevitable face plant...in the sand. In Psalm 73, Asaph sounds just about as confused. Life isn't fair. God seems silent. Asaph is befuddled. Jaded. Tossed and turned by waves of hurt and frustration.

In the Word

Read Psalm 73 today and pay special attention to verses 12-14:

This is what the wicked are like—always carefree, they go on amassing wealth. Surely in vain I have kept my heart pure and have washed my hands in innocence. All day long I have been afflicted, and every morning brings new punishments.

Why? It's a question we all ask when life isn't the way we think it's supposed to be. In Psalm 73, Asaph gets gut-honest with God. It sounds like some of my discussions with God:

I know God is good, but I've lost my foothold.
I'm tumbled in the waves of doubt.

61

I don't even know what's real anymore. I just hurt.
And when I try to talk to God, it doesn't seem like he's
   even there.
All I hear is silence. It doesn't make sense to me:
the prideful, selfish people I know seem to be living the
   dream.
And me? I'm trying to follow God, and my life is so hard.
Why would God do this to me? It makes me angry.
Kind of bitter, actually. I feel confused.
But, God, I know you are real, and that you never change.
You're always with me…even now when it doesn't
   make sense.

When we suffer heartache, our first reaction is often, "This isn't fair!" Depending on the cause, we may be exactly right. In Psalm 73, Asaph looked around and saw that wicked people were happy and successful, but he endured hardship even though he tried his best to follow God. He accused God of not caring, but eventually, God opened Asaph's eyes to the reality of God's justice: *Even though life isn't fair, God is sovereign, and he is working for my good.*

Why do bad things happen to us? This was Asaph's question; maybe it's yours. When we're hurt, we often try to find the cause. Stop and think. What might have caused your brokenness?

- *Our own sins and foolish decisions.* Because of the fall, we make foolish, self-destructive, and selfish choices that cause us and God heartache. Like Adam, we pass blame to others ("She made me do it") or to God ("You gave her to me. It's your fault!").

- *Other people's sins that wound us.* Adam and Eve's family experienced sibling rivalry that ended in murder. Not a great beginning! Many of us have suffered verbal, physical, or sexual abuse. We feel furious and lonely, afraid and desperately needy. And rightly so.

- *Spiritual conflict.* The enemy of our souls uses temptation,

accusation, and deception to get us off God's path and
cause us to doubt God's purposes for us. In most cases,
the battle is waged in our minds, where truth is our most
potent weapon.

- *God's discipline.* Some of the pain we experience is God's
  way of getting our attention to correct our wayward-
  ness, just like a loving father disciplines his children—for
  our good.

- *This fallen world.* One natural disaster can wreck a life…
  and a family. This can include environmental disasters (like a hurricane) or personal disasters (like health
  problems).

We may not have an answer to the question of "why?" in this life.
But in Isaiah 45:6-7, God makes it clear who's in charge: "I am the
LORD, and there is no other. I form the light and create darkness, I
bring prosperity and create disaster; I, the LORD, do all these things."

Make It Real

Brokenness cries out for healing. Instead of self-medicating our
pain, we need to allow God to carry us through it. Maybe you're hurting right now because of a foolish choice you made. Or because of the
evil someone else did to you. Maybe there's not any simple explanation,
except that we live in a fallen, broken, messed-up world.

Regardless of the "why," hear this: God wants to reveal himself to
you in a new way. If you've sinned, God wants to forgive you and give
you a fresh start. If you've been wronged by someone else, he wants to
hold you and cry with you in your pain. If your heart is screaming "why?"
about a great loss, God wants to tell you, "I know this hurts, but I've got
you. I love you. I'm not leaving and we will get through this…together."

In what area of your life is it most difficult to trust God and rest in
him? Why?

Kids + grand kids
because I care so deeply &
desperately for their welfare &
good

Can you identify any of the causes of the hardships you've experienced in recent years?

How has God revealed himself to you through hardship?

Take a moment to read each one of these verses and think about how they apply to your life. Wherever you can do it, insert your name in the verses. Pray these passages over your heart.

- "My help comes from the LORD, the Maker of heaven and earth" (Psalm 121:2).
- "Do not fear, for I have redeemed you; I have summoned you by name; you are mine" (Isaiah 43:1).

Heart to Heart

Okay, so I can be a bit emotional sometimes (just ask Tim). Every woman has her bad days…and PMS doesn't help. Even when we *know* truths about God—that he's loving, good, and faithful—we just want to make sense out of all the confusion. And right now! When we aren't facing big life trials, there are many daily frustrations that send us into an emotional tailspin.

It's important and healthy for us to realize that we can't and shouldn't measure God's goodness by our current emotional state. If your life feels out of control, remember that God is *in* control. Proverbs 3:5 says, "Trust in the LORD with all your heart." It means to be bold. Confident. Secure. To rest in him. How can you rest in the Lord today?

⁓

God, the waves are relentless. My strength is gone and I feel like I am drowning. Rescue me and give me strength to hold to everything I know about you…even when I can't see you.

Day 4

Nothing Wasted

*Your most profound and intimate experiences of worship
will likely be in your darkest days...when your heart is
broken, when you feel abandoned, when you are out of
options, when the pain is great, and you turn to God alone.*

RICK WARREN

God never wastes our pain. He is gracious and wise to use it, if we'll let him, to grow and change us. The apostle Paul's life wasn't exactly easy...jail time, a shipwreck, being stoned. But somehow, in the midst of his hardship, Paul found God and experienced joy.

In the Word

Read Romans 5:1-11 today and pay special attention to verses 3-5:

> *We also glory in our sufferings, because we know that suffering produces perseverance; perseverance, character; and character, hope. And hope does not put us to shame, because God's love has been poured out into our hearts through the Holy Spirit, who has been given to us.*

Often, the good God produces through our suffering doesn't miraculously change the situation, but changes us. That's what Paul is talking about in this passage. Notice the progression. At first, all we can do is hang on and not let go, but as we keep trusting God, he transforms our character, and the fruit of the Spirit is formed in us more fully than ever before.

Gradually, we come to believe—truly believe—that God is at work behind the scenes and is accomplishing something more wonderful than we ever imagined. As faith and hope become firmly rooted we sense God's abundant love even in the middle of our continued struggle.

I believe God uses difficulties far more than pleasant times to shape our lives. In the crucible of doubt and discouragement, we cling to God, search his word for answers, talk to wise friends, and depend on his Spirit to guide us. And in those times, we cast off old habits and try new things. These experiences, then, can bring out the very best in us. Gerald May wisely observed,

> In reality, our lack of fulfillment is the most precious gift we have. It is the source of our passion, our creativity, our search for God. All the best of life comes out of our human yearning—our not being satisfied.[1]

Make It Real

Some of us look at life through rose-colored glasses, but many of us major on the minors and neglect to care about the things that break God's heart. Suffering changes that; it clarifies our vision. As C.S. Lewis put it, "[Pain] is God's megaphone to rouse a deaf world."[2] We begin to realize what's really important, what's worthy of our concern, and what has been a meaningless distraction.

The experience of suffering also teaches us to treasure each moment of every day. Walter Ciszek dreamed of being a missionary in Russia, but he was assigned to Poland. During World War II, he was captured and put in solitary confinement in Moscow for five torturous years. He was sent to a Siberian labor camp, where prisoners worked from sunup to sundown every day. For a while, Ciszek felt sorry for himself and angry with God. Then, he realized that God had given him a place—in Russia—to serve people who desperately needed his help. Reflecting on this new faith in God, he wrote:

> Each day should be more than an obstacle to be gotten over, a span of time to be endured, a sequence of hours to be survived. For me, each day came forth from the hand of

God, newly created and alive with opportunities to do his
will…We can accept and offer back to God every prayer,
work, and suffering of the day, no matter how insignificant
or unspectacular they may seem to us.[3]

If "pain is God's megaphone," what is God saying to you through
your pain and hardship?

What would you say are the biggest lessons God has taught you
through suffering?

Revisit Romans 5:3-5. Describe the sequence of growth in this passage.

Like Walter Ciszek, how can you see God's working in the midst of
your brokenness?

Take a moment to read each one of these verses and think about
how they apply to your life. Wherever you can do it, insert your name
in the verses. Pray these passages over your heart.

- "Come to me, all you who are weary and burdened,
  and I will give you rest. Take my yoke upon you and learn
  from me, for I am gentle and humble in heart, and you
  will find rest for your souls" (Matthew 11:28-29).

- "I consider that our present sufferings are not worth
  comparing with the glory that will be revealed in us"
  (Romans 8:18).

- "But he said to me, 'My grace is sufficient for you, for my power is made perfect in weakness.' Therefore I will boast all the more gladly about my weaknesses, so that Christ's power may rest upon me" (2 Corinthians 12:9).

Heart to Heart

One of my favorite quotations about healing is by professor and author Dan Allender. He describes true, heart healing this way:

> Suffering need not destroy the heart; it has the potential to lead to life…But few of us enter the tragedy of living in a fallen world and simultaneously struggle with God until our hearts bleed with hope…Healing in this life is not the *resolution* of our past; it is the *use* of our past to draw us into deeper relationship with God and his purposes for our lives.[4]

I'm afraid many of us never learn the deep, rich lessons God wants to teach us through our pain. We just want relief. The courageous among us, though, look beyond our pain to find the hands and the face of God.

There, we open our hearts to experience his goodness and greatness more deeply than ever before. I'm learning to pray, "Lord, what do you want me to learn through this?" rather than just "Lord, fix it!"

Father, my desire is to be perfect and complete in you,
lacking nothing. I am learning that my pain and trials
can be used by you to strengthen me. God, give me freedom
to be weak and to invite you into my weakness.

Day 5

Wounded Healers

*God uses broken things. It takes broken soil to produce
a crop, broken clouds to give rain, broken grain to
give bread, broken bread to give strength. It is the
broken alabaster box that gives forth perfume.*

VANCE HAVNER

God's desire for you, his daughter, is not just to be healed, but to become a healer. Sure, you will carry scars for the rest of your life. Scars, not gaping wounds. Scars that are a testimony to the love of God that is stronger than your pain...a love that never gives up, even when you want to. That's the Gospel. Wounded, but healed. Healed to be a wounded healer.

In the Word

Read 2 Corinthians 1:1-11 today and pay special attention to verses 3-4:

> *Praise be to the God and Father of our Lord Jesus Christ, the Father of compassion and the God of all comfort, who comforts us in all our troubles, so that we can comfort those in any trouble with the comfort we ourselves receive from God.*

If you believe in Jesus, you'll have a dream life. God will bless you with a big house. A nice car. A successful career. A happy marriage. Well-behaved kids. Two weeks of vacation every year. An early retirement. And of course, a long life. At least that's what some churches—and Christian authors—are saying these days.

There's a lot of talk about "God's favor," "God's blessing," and "God's smile." And frankly, sometimes I wonder what Bible these folks are reading. When I read God's Word, it seems to me that, as Christians, life involves hardship, suffering, pain, and loss. Jesus himself said, "In this world you will have trouble." But he adds, "Take heart! I have overcome the world" (John 16:33).

James echoes this when he writes, "Consider it pure joy, my brothers and sisters, whenever you face trials of many kinds" (James 1:2).

It's always dangerous when we begin to think that God exists to make us happy. To give us what we want. To make life easy. There's a danger to this kind of mindset. When hardship comes, we feel like God is being unjust or cruel to us. That he's ignoring us. Let's look for a minute at Paul's experience. Fill in the blanks from 2 Corinthians 1:9-10:

"We felt we had received the sentence of _death_. But this happened that we might not rely on _ourselves_ but on _God_, who raises the dead. He has delivered us from such a deadly peril, and he will deliver us again. On him we have set our hope."

Not exactly a walk in the park, is it? The daily reality of Paul's life was very hard...maybe harder than you or I could imagine.

Make It Real

You and I were never created for this fallen world. We were made for Eden...and heaven. And that's why I love verse 4: "God...comforts us in all our troubles."

What's that word? *In.* In our troubles. There's no guarantee that just because we believe in God, life will be easy. Not at all! But we do have the confidence of knowing that God is with us in our troubles. Sometimes, we don't have an end to the pain in our lives. Sometimes, it goes on. Sometimes, it's not just brokenness that hurts. Healing hurts, too.

The experiences of your life and mine influence who we become. Over the years, I've had the privilege of talking with hundreds of women who have turned their traumatic experiences of suffering into a platform to serve, help, and care for others who are hurting. I love these women. My life is richer because I know them. I have great respect for their courage and compassion for others. They are heroines of the faith. Author and pastor Henri Nouwen called them "wounded healers."[1] Many of these women have shared remarkable truths about their pain:

"Julie, if I could live my life over again, I don't know if I would change that hardship."

"I wouldn't be the woman I am today, without wrestling through that."

"I wouldn't know God in such a personal, intimate way if my life had been easy."

"I wouldn't have gotten to see God provide for me in such a powerful way."

"I wouldn't have compassion for other people without having journeyed through the pain."

Granted, our human perspective is limited. But these women have found a deeper purpose to their times of trouble. One of those purposes is: "So that we can comfort those in any trouble with the comfort we ourselves receive from God."

How has the pain and brokenness in your life changed your view of life? God? Yourself?

Reread the focus verse. Describe in your own words what it means to become a wounded healer.

Who do you know who is a model of a wounded healer? Describe this person's character and role of providing comfort to others.

Are you a wounded healer? If so, how is God using you?

Take a moment to read each one of these verses and think about how they apply to your life. Wherever you can do it, insert your name in the verses. Pray these passages over your heart.

- "But you, Lord, are a compassionate and gracious God, slow to anger, abounding in love and faithfulness" (Psalm 86:15).

- "Now to him who is able to do immeasurably more than all we ask or imagine, according to his power that is at work within us" (Ephesians 3:20).

Heart to Heart

As you and I experience healing, God may bless us with the opportunity to walk with others in their pain. However, we must avoid the compulsion to act as heroes and try to fix others' problems. Healing is about God, not us! The need to "fix" suggests that our souls are still wounded. Don't be surprised if you find this motive in your heart. We're all still works in progress.

We have a profound responsibility to be Christ's hands to touch lives with his love, but we can't make people respond, grow, and heal. They have to find the courage to take their own steps. One of our chief goals, then, is to know where our responsibility stops and theirs starts. If we cross that line, we're hindering their progress, not helping them.

Author and therapist Daphne Rose Kingma challenges us, "Today see if you can stretch your heart and expand your love so that it touches not only those to whom you can give it easily but also those who need it so much."[2] One measure of our love is our willingness to care for people who aren't very attractive to us: the whining, griping, passive, angry, and annoying people we try to avoid.

Give because so much has been given to you, love because you know what it's like for one who was rejected to now be accepted, and open your heart to those who can hardly believe there's anyone they can trust. This is true soul care.

⌒

*Lord, thank you for the times in my life when I have hurt...
and for the healing you have brought. Help me in turn to
comfort others with the comfort that you have given me.*

Week 4

Extraordinary Forgiveness:
From Guilt to Grace

[forgiveness:] cancelling the debt of another
person's wrong and setting myself free to love

S ince that tragic day in the Garden, sin has plagued every person
who has walked the planet. To cope with the reality of our sin, we
come up with all kinds of creative plans: excusing ourselves, blaming
others, insisting it wasn't that bad, or saying it never happened at all.

The consequences of sin are all around us. Individuals, families, and
friends are devastated by its toxic power. But God offers forgiveness—
full and free—to anyone bold enough to take him up on his invitation.

This week, we'll explore two women who experienced the shame
of their selfishness—Miriam and the woman caught in adultery—and
we'll look at some very important passages of Scripture to help us experience and express God's magnificent gift of forgiveness.

Day 1

Miriam's Mess-up

*To forgive is to set a prisoner free
and discover that the prisoner was you.*

LEWIS B. SMEDES

Understanding forgiveness starts with seeing how God relates to us. Every day, God gives us grace and forgiveness that we don't deserve. Forgiving doesn't minimize wrongdoing. And it doesn't magically clear up consequences. Miriam's disobedience resulted in leprosy, and there are definite consequences to our pride and selfishness, too. But forgiveness does *set us free.*

In the Word

Read Numbers 12 today and pay special attention to verses 1-2:

> *Miriam and Aaron began to talk against Moses because of his Cushite wife..."Has the LORD spoken only through Moses?" they asked. "Hasn't he also spoken through us?"*

Miriam and Aaron had a front row seat to watch God work miracles through their brother Moses as he confronted Pharaoh and freed the captive Israelites. Moses had been chosen by God to lead the people, maybe two million strong, out of Egypt toward the Promised Land. But sibling rivalry operates in every culture and in every era, and these two couldn't stand their brother's popularity. They wanted a share of his fame, so they publicly cut Moses down. Lowering him, they figured, would elevate them to his status.

It's easy to hurt other people with our cutting remarks. Our cold shoulders. Our calloused hearts. And often our motivation is to improve our standing among others and to preserve our pride. Have you ever had a Miriam moment? You said something that didn't need to be said—that shouldn't have been said?

The people weren't the only ones who heard the jealous siblings complain. God heard them, too. God called the three together and spoke to them out of a pillar of cloud. His anger burned and he pronounced judgment. The leader of the rebellion, Miriam, became snow-white with leprosy. In Miriam's world, a leper was an outcast.

If that were the end of the story, we'd be tempted to label God as cruel and harsh, even though, in reality, God was acting out of justice by punishing sin. But, thankfully, it's not the end of the story or the lesson. Grab your Bible and flip over to Exodus 34:6-7. Fill in the blanks to see how God describes himself:

> The LORD, the LORD, the *Compassionate* and gracious God,
> slow to anger, abounding in love and *faithfulness*
> maintaining love to thousands, and *forgiving*
> wickedness, rebellion and sin.

Our God is a God of justice and mercy. He forgives. It's impossible to understand true forgiveness without going back to where it all starts: *God's forgiveness*. Miriam had rebelled against Moses…and against God. Outside the camp, she got what she deserved. Public shame. Separation from God's people. Disgrace. But forgiveness isn't about giving people what they deserve. It's about redemption. It's about extending grace… what people don't deserve.

Miriam was exiled outside the camp for seven days to atone for her sin, but Jesus willingly chose to suffer. Not to atone for his sins, but to atone for *my* sins. Your sins.

The Bible says that "Jesus also suffered outside the city gate to make the people holy through his own blood" (Hebrews 13:12). You and I have already been forgiven because of the sacrifice of Jesus. Because we have been forgiven, we can, in turn, forgive.

Make It Real

We'd like to think forgiveness wipes out every consequence of our sins, but that's not quite the case. Often, we experience painful results of our pride and selfishness as a reminder to us (and to those who observe us) that sin is serious business. God's miracle is that he forgives, restores, and uses our experience to teach us valuable lessons.

Being real about forgiveness requires that we be frank about our sins. It's not easy to be ruthlessly honest about the darkness in our hearts, but it's essential. As we experience God's cleansing of our own sins, we'll be much more willing and able to forgive those who hurt us.

For many women, forgiveness is the pivotal issue of their lives. They've been deeply wounded by abuse, betrayal, or divorce, and they can't seem to get beyond their all-consuming pain. It colors every desire and every relationship. And here's a key point: Your past isn't your past if it is still affecting your present. Learning the principles of forgiveness—and mustering the courage to choose to forgive—sets us free in ways we never imagined.

The process of uncovering our pain and resentment can be excruciating. We all need a faithful friend to walk those paths with us. As we cross barriers of bitterness, resentment, and self-protection, the journey leads to freedom, joy, wisdom, and love. As one poet put it: "Where there is ruin, there is chance to find treasure." Part of that treasure is forgiveness. And freedom.

> When people aren't completely honest about their sins (public and private, horrible and culturally acceptable), how might they think about God's forgiveness?

> Read Numbers 12:1-15. Does it diminish God's forgiveness and restoration to read that Miriam suffered consequences for her sin of envy and rebellion? Why or why not?

> What are some of the lessons we learn—the treasures we find—by being honest about our sins, experiencing consequences, and finding freedom and relief in God's grace?

Take a moment to read each one of these verses and think about how they apply to your life. Wherever you can do it, insert your name in the verses. Pray these passages over your heart.

- "I, even I, am he who blots out your transgressions, for my own sake, and remembers your sins no more" (Isaiah 43:25).

- "My dear children, I write this to you so that you will not sin. But if anybody does sin, we have an advocate with the Father—Jesus Christ, the Righteous One" (1 John 2:1).

Heart to Heart

Joe Stowell, the former president of Moody Bible Institute, once wrote, "To think that we haven't been saved from much leaves us feeling we really haven't been forgiven much."[1] Jesus told his disciples the same thing in Luke 7. Sometimes it would bother me that I didn't have the powerful "saved out of drugs, alcohol, and crazy rebellion" testimony that some women have and can say, "Isn't God awesome?"

Then it dawned on me…some of us were saved out of that lifestyle. Others of us were saved *from* that lifestyle. But we all have one thing in common: Paul says in Ephesians 2 that we are all children of darkness and spiritually dead—in need of redemption through Jesus' blood, the forgiveness of our trespasses according to the riches of his grace—which he *lavished* on all of us.

That's grace…and that's forgiveness.

⌐

God, today's prayer is simple. Thank you for your forgiveness.
I don't deserve it, but I wouldn't want to live without it.

Day 2

Caught!

Either sin is with you, lying on your shoulders, or it is lying on Christ, the Lamb of God. Now if it is lying on your back, you are lost; but if it is resting on Christ, you are free, and you will be saved. Now choose what you want.

MARTIN LUTHER

There's nothing more embarrassing than being caught red-handed in a sin. In the moment, we often respond by justifying our behavior. Minimizing our guilt. Making excuses. "I couldn't stop myself" or "It's not *that* bad" or "The serpent deceived me, and I ate." But the guilt remains. And even if no one ever finds out, our secrets can eat us alive. For the woman in today's story, getting caught wasn't just humiliating. It meant being stoned to death. Until Jesus showed up...

In the Word

Read John 8:1-11 today and pay special attention to verses 3-5:

> *The teachers of the law and the Pharisees brought in a woman caught in adultery. They made her stand before the group and said to Jesus, "Teacher, this woman was caught in the act of adultery. In the Law Moses commanded us to stone such women. Now what do you say?"*

In Jesus' day, men could get away with almost anything, but women who committed sexual indiscretions were publicly stoned to death. John tells us about a moment when the religious leaders brought to Jesus a woman who had been caught in the act of adultery. (I'm not sure what they were doing standing outside the door, and there's no mention of how they dealt with the man, but those are questions for another day.)

I can imagine how they treated this woman. The men probably weren't respectful or gentle in any way. They likely threw her clothes at her, and as she fumbled to put them on, they grabbed her by the arm and yanked her down the street half-naked. They didn't worry about bruises. The stones would make far more dramatic marks on her.

The men dragged the woman in front of Jesus and asked him, "You know what the Law of Moses says about women caught in adultery. She should die! What do you say we should do?" They wanted to see if the forgiveness Jesus talked about superseded Old Testament law.

And Jesus did something very strange. He bent down and wrote in the sand. Impatient, the men kept asking him the same question. Then, John tells us, "He straightened up and said to them, 'Let any one of you who is without sin be the first to throw a stone at her.'"

Ouch! Slowly, the accusers walked away, one by one. These men realized that they, too, were sinful. Before long, Jesus stood in the street with this woman…alone.

Can you imagine her shock and relief? Especially when she heard these words: "Neither do I condemn you. Go now and leave your life of sin."

Make It Real

Any one of us would dread being caught in our sins, whatever they may be. We're afraid that someday, somehow, someone will see us deeply enmeshed in our sin, and we'll experience the shame of public exposure. This story shows us that Jesus isn't harsh and angry. In fact, he loves us so much that he gave his own life to forgive us and restore us. Jesus desires that you and I have the courage to admit our sins to him so that we, too, can bask in his cleansing love and grace.

The sins we cover, God will uncover. The sins we uncover, God will cover. I've talked to many brave women who had the courage to be honest about their sins, but still couldn't believe that God would forgive them. Maybe a past abortion. Adultery. Or an unbiblical divorce. Through tears, these women said, "Yes Julie, I know he will forgive *those* people for what they've done, but not me. His grace is for others. I'm afraid it's not for me."

But God's forgiveness is for you. For me. For every one of us. The law condemned this woman, and society demanded retribution, but Jesus treated her with love, respect, and grace. He didn't excuse her behavior, and he didn't sanction it in the future. But his words set her free: *I, the God of the universe, do not condemn you. I forgive your sin. So don't live in shame or fear. Go, and sin no more.*

There is no sin so great that God's grace is not greater still. God's forgiveness changes lives. It frees us from the guilt and shame of our pasts. The power of grace reshaped this woman's choices in the future.

How do you feel when you're "caught in the act"? How do you typically respond in those moments?

Read Romans 8:1. On a scale of 0 (not in the least) to 10 (completely), how much do you really believe God's forgiveness wipes away all condemnation from you?

If you had been the woman in John 8, how would this encounter with Jesus have changed the direction of your life?

Take a moment to read each one of these verses and think about how they apply to your life. Wherever you can do it, insert your name in the verses. Pray these passages over your heart.

- "'Come now, let us settle the matter,' says the Lord.
  'Though your sins are like scarlet, they shall be as white as snow'" (Isaiah 1:18).

- "Repent, then, and turn to God, so that your sins may be

wiped out, that times of refreshing may come from the
Lord" (Acts 3:19).

- "If we confess our sins, he is faithful and just and will forgive us our sins and purify us from all unrighteousness"
(1 John 1:9).

Heart to Heart

I'll never forget walking into the kitchen one afternoon to find my
son, Zach, up on the counter, stuffing his little face with cookies I had
just baked—the kind with M&Ms, his favorite. The sight of my little
man caught rainbow-handed was so comical, I wasn't sure whether
to laugh or scold him. I'm sure many emotions flew through him in
that instant!

Shame. Guilt. Fear. Ever feel like you have been caught, revealed,
uncovered? I have! These feelings crowd our minds when our sin is
exposed. God's heart and hope is that the conviction we feel will spring-
board us into his forgiveness. But too often, I camp there in my sense of
humiliation, unworthiness, and disgrace. I get stuck in my emotional
pit, and in that place it's easy to begin believing Satan's lies. *God would
never—could never—forgive you. And if your friends, your family…if they
knew? They'd reject you for sure. Not even a question.*

As you grapple with the reality of God's forgiveness in your life,
fight your doubts with the promises of God's Word. Even when you
don't *feel* forgiven, the truth is that, in Jesus, you are forgiven. And
nothing can ever change that. Accepting and living in God's forgiveness frees us to become extraordinary women!

⌒

*Lord, you know the deepest, darkest parts of my heart. Nothing is
hidden from your sight. Even when I try to hide my sin from you,
you see it. And yet, somehow…you still love me! Free me from the
condemnation I feel and open my heart to your forgiveness for me.*

Day 3

We Are All Prodigals

*Jesus Christ...saw us enslaved by the very things we
thought would free us...At the cost of his life, [Jesus]
paid the debt for our sins, purchasing us the only
place our hearts can rest, in his Father's house.*

TIM KELLER

Our grasp of sin and our grasp of forgiveness go hand in hand. Let's be honest: We are all prodigals. We all want our own way or the highway, and left to ourselves, we'd probably end up not too far from the pigpen, filling our hearts with garbage, and wondering why we're not satisfied. Jesus' parable of the prodigal son is more than just a story in the Bible. It's our story.

In the Word

Read Luke 15:11-32 today and pay special attention to verses 18-20:

> *"I will set out and go back to my father and say to him: 'Father,
> I have sinned against heaven and against you. I am no longer
> worthy to be called your son; make me like one of your hired
> servants.' So he got up and went to his father.*

The prodigal son felt completely justified by demanding his share of the inheritance (while his father was still living) and leaving home to go "live it up." In Jewish culture, this was equivalent to saying, "Dad, I wish you were dead." He couldn't have dishonored his father more by his attitude and behavior, but, in the moment, only one thing mattered.

Being happy. Having fun. At our worst moments, we, like the prodigal, care only about our own pleasure, popularity, and possessions. Thoughts of others are far from our minds. But such self-serving living never pays off. Leave God out of the picture, and eventually our plans and dreams will crash and burn. When this man was penniless, he got a job feeding pigs, a forbidden animal in the Jewish culture. He hit rock bottom. What about for you? Maybe it's confusion. Dissatisfaction. A loveless marriage. A job you hate. Or just an aching longing in your soul for something more.

Finally, the young man came to his senses about his sins and decided to go back home. He didn't believe he deserved to be forgiven and reinstated by his father, so he planned to ask if he could simply be a servant on the family farm. When his father saw him coming down the road, however, he did the last thing the prodigal expected.

He abandoned all dignity and ran. He threw his arms around him. Kissed him. Before the boy could even get his confession out, the father put new clothes in his hand and started the party planning to celebrate: "For [he] was dead and is alive again; he was lost and is found."

But it all began in the stench of the pigpen, with heartfelt honesty and confession.

Make It Real

If we're not aware of the depths of our sins, we won't appreciate God's forgiveness nearly as much. Does the fact that God knows everything—absolutely everything—about you comfort you or terrify you? Maybe both, depending on the circumstances. Being real in our relationship with God means that we respond when his Spirit taps us on the shoulder and says, "That attitude was wrong," or "The words you just said were meant to hurt instead of heal, and that's sin."

We sometimes think of forgiveness as a judicial act by God to declare us "not guilty." It's that, but it's also more. As Luke's illustration shows, forgiveness restores our relationship with God. God, the righteous judge, demanded the penalty be paid for our sins, but he accepted Jesus as our substitute.

In an incredible act of grace, he invites us to join his own family...

not as a hired servant, but as a child. A daughter. And here's the wild part: The more we are convinced that God's forgiveness is full, free, and refreshing—not a scam or an abstract idea—the more we can open our hearts and be honest about the dark things we've locked inside. As we bring our secrets out, bit by bit, into the light of God's love and grace, we'll find him to be just like the prodigal's dad—not reluctant or slow to forgive—but thrilled to celebrate his forgiveness with us!

Read Psalm 139:1-4. Does the fact that God knows everything about you comfort you or terrify you? Explain your answer.

Is it hard for you to understand God as a loving, pursuing, forgiving father? Why?

As you've read today's lesson, have any long-buried sins come to mind that need to be confessed and forgiven? Take some time now to confess them to God and experience his forgiveness and healing.

Take a moment to read each one of these verses and think about how they apply to your life. Wherever you can do it, insert your name in the verses. Pray these passages over your heart.

- "In him we have redemption through his blood, the forgiveness of sins, in accordance with the riches of God's grace" (Ephesians 1:7).

- "The Lord our God is merciful and forgiving, even though we have rebelled against him" (Daniel 9:9).

- "As far as the east is from the west, so far has he removed our transgressions from us" (Psalm 103:12).

Heart to Heart

One of my favorite verses is from Colossians 1: "For he has rescued us from the dominion of darkness and brought us into the kingdom of the Son he loves, in whom we have redemption, the forgiveness of sins" (Colossians 1:13-14).

As a little girl, I always imagined myself as a princess, the daughter of a king. I lived in a castle. And someday, my prince would come.

This verse refers to a kingdom, too. The dominion of darkness. Not exactly my fairy tale, but Paul describes how you and I and every person on this earth was a slave to sin. Until our rescuer came. Through his sacrifice on the cross, Jesus has brought us into the kingdom of his Father. And that's not all! He's also given us redemption. Forgiveness. And the privilege of being his daughter—his princess. Fairy tales come true. That's worth celebrating!

Lord, I'm overwhelmed by the fact that you know me completely and still extend forgiveness to me. Thank you for running after and pursuing me, even when I sin and fail you. Shine the light of your truth into the dark places of my heart. Show me how much I need you.

Day 4

Poison in the Soul

Forgiveness is the key that unlocks the door of resentment and the handcuffs of hate. It is a power that breaks the chains of bitterness and the shackles of selfishness.

WILLIAM ARTHUR WARD

It's been said that choosing to hold onto a grudge is like drinking poison and expecting the other person to die. Poison kills. Bitterness is the poison that kills our hearts. That's why we can never let bitterness put down roots in our lives.

In the Word

Read Ephesians 4:17-32 today and pay special attention to verses 31-32:

> *Get rid of all bitterness, rage and anger, brawling and slander, along with every form of malice. Be kind and compassionate to one another, forgiving each other, just as in Christ God forgave you.*

A rude remark. An insensitive comment. Being taken for granted. Or worse, being ignored and forgotten by someone we thought cared about us. It's impossible to go through life (and maybe even a day) without being hurt by someone, whether they mean to or not.

We can resolve most of these situations with a little communication and a dab of grace. But many of us have experienced deeper wounds that have never healed. Unresolved hurt and anger don't just melt away.

They fester, and they poison every part of our lives. Soon, bitterness takes root in our hearts and consumes us.

In Ephesians 4, Paul challenges us to deal ruthlessly with our bitterness and replace it with kindness, compassion, and forgiveness. Why? Because bitterness pollutes our perspective and steals our joy. The idea of "get rid" is similar to *casting off*, as you would your dirty clothes after a long day of yard work, and *releasing*, as you would set down the grocery bags with a sigh when you finally made it up the front steps and into the kitchen!

Overcoming bitterness is both a choice and a process. The process of grief is critical in order to come to grips with the reality of the loss, to truly forgive those who hurt us, and learn new skills in relationships so that we aren't demanding or vulnerable any longer. I don't believe people can resolve deep and long-lasting bitterness on their own...or overnight. They need a godly, committed friend to walk with them. As you read this, you may realize you are one who needs to take the first steps down that path, or you may know others who need your help to face the inevitable obstacles on their path to freedom.

Before we begin to address the reality of bitterness in our lives, we often feel completely justified in our resentment. After all, that person hurt us, and he's not even sorry about it! As we move forward, though, all the painful emotions we've kept in check now flood our hearts, and it really hurts. That's when we need a friend to hold our hand and tell us, "This is normal. You're going to be all right. Let's keep walking together."

Make It Real

Bitterness gives us two things that shape our lives: identity and energy. We see ourselves as "the one who was wronged," and we get an adrenaline rush each day from the emotional intensity of our resentment. This identity, though, makes us demand that others treat us perfectly and that no one ever hurt us again. That's an unreasonable demand, and those unrealistic expectations lead to even more hurt, anger, and resentment. Author and pastor Frederick Buechner chillingly describes the consequences of harboring bitterness:

> To lick your wounds, to smack your lips over grievances long past, to roll over your tongue the prospect of bitter confrontations still to come, to savor to the last toothsome morsel…the pain you are giving back—in many ways it is a feast fit for a king. The chief drawback is that what you're wolfing down is yourself. The skeleton at the feast is you![1]

Doctors report that as many as 70 percent of medical office visits are for psychosomatic illness directly traced to bitterness and resentment. Divorce courts are filled with couples who never resolved the hurts they inflicted on each other, and countless couples and their children live in an armed truce waiting for one side to start shooting. When we let bitterness grow inside, our list of wrongs inevitably continues to grow, and we often grow angry at God, too.

How does bitterness poison our lives physically, mentally, relationally, and spiritually?

Reread Ephesians 4:31-32. In what ways is overcoming bitterness a choice? A process?

Do you need to address bitterness in your own heart, or do you have a friend who needs your help to take these steps? What's your next step?

Take a moment to read each one of these verses and think about how they apply to your life. Wherever you can do it, insert your name in the verses. Pray these passages over your heart.

- "Make every effort to live in peace with everyone….See

to it that no one falls short of the grace of God and that no bitter root grows up to cause trouble and defile many" (Hebrews 12:14-15).

- "Everyone should be quick to listen, slow to speak and slow to become angry, because human anger does not produce the righteousness that God desires" (James 1:19-20).

Heart to Heart

Relationships are one of life's greatest challenges. And when you live with someone, you see the good, the bad, and the ugly. It hasn't been an easy road for Tim and me. Especially the first few years! We said and did things that were hurtful. I remember thinking during one argument, "Enough is enough. I don't want to do this anymore. I'm out of here!"

When we feel scared and unloved, it takes a lot of grace to face our fears. Our natural response is to withdraw from the problem, blame the other person, and walk away. During that argument I realized the truth: it takes two. I was wrong too, not just Tim. Ouch.

To forgive is to release the hurt. To let the past be past. To extend grace. To cast off bitterness and choose to love. I'm not saying that being honest about the pain someone has inflicted on us is easy. It's incredibly difficult to face horrible wounds some of us have experienced, but it's necessary if we want to live in freedom.

Don't let bitterness poison your soul and every relationship in your life. Be honest about what happened, how you felt then, and how you feel now. And choose to forgive. Grieving takes time, so be patient. God smiles on you each step of the way.

Lord, please show me any bitterness I'm holding onto. I realize how damaging it is, and I don't want to live this way. Open my eyes to see people the way you see them. Open my heart to extend your grace to them, even when I've been hurt and wronged.

Day 5

Forgiveness and Trust

Forgiveness is letting go of the past.
Trust has to do with future behavior.
RICK WARREN

orgive. One simple, little, ordinary word. One word that's incredibly hard to actually *live*. When I'm hurt, everything in me wants to hurt back. Or at least show *them* what it feels like. C'mon, let's be honest. Forgiveness isn't easy. It's not fun. It doesn't feel normal. But when we choose to release our hurt to God, to let him be in charge of revenge-giving, we free ourselves.

In the Word

Read Matthew 5:43-48 today and pay special attention to verses 43-45:

> *"You have heard that it was said, 'Love your neighbor and hate your enemy.' But I tell you, love your enemies and pray for those who persecute you, that you may be children of your Father in heaven."*

Forgiveness isn't saying "it's no big deal." Forgiveness says, "You hurt me. A lot. And I still hurt, but I am choosing to let go of my burning desire to get you back—to hurt you in turn. I choose to extend grace to you, because God has poured out his grace on me. I choose to release my anger and grudge to God, so I don't need to hold this against you anymore."

In Matthew 5, Jesus says something extremely radical. *Forgive…love…pray for your enemies*. What do you think that means? What would it look like for you to love the "enemies" in your life?

In my conversations with women around the country, I've noticed that many of us confuse forgiveness and trust. "If I forgive the person who hurt me so badly," they assume, "I'll have to trust him. I just can't do that, so I'll avoid the risk by not forgiving him in the first place."

There are many reasons people refuse to forgive those who offend them, including:

- He isn't sorry for what he did.
- She'll just do it again, so why bother?
- It wasn't an accident. He meant it!
- How can I forgive something like that?
- I can't forgive because I'm still so hurt and angry. I'd be a hypocrite.

What are some reasons that make it hard for you to forgive others? Forgiving those who hurt us is difficult. Philip Yancey called it "the unnatural act"[1] because it flies in the face of our desire for revenge. Similarly, C.S. Lewis wrote, "Every one says forgiveness is a lovely idea, until they have something to forgive."[2] One of the main reasons we refuse to forgive is that we falsely believe we have to immediately begin trusting the person who hurt us. I have news for you: That's just not true.

Forgiveness takes one. We are commanded by God to forgive unilaterally, whether the other person is sorry, repents, meant to do it, or did something intentionally horrific. We forgive in order to resolve the hurt and anger inside us and to express the forgiveness we've experienced from God.

But trust takes two. Trust isn't unilateral. Rebuilding a relationship takes both parties earning each other's trust with consistently honorable actions over time. It's entirely possible—and in some cases, necessary—to forgive someone but not trust him.

Make It Real

As we discuss forgiveness today, I'm not talking about forgiving the barista for making your soy latte with skim or your kids for not picking up the toys. That's one thing. But how are we to extend forgiveness in relationships that have been broken by betrayal, abuse, or abandonment?

When Jesus sent his followers out to spread the gospel, he knew they would be tested by the reactions of people in the cities. Some people would respect them, but some would abuse them. So he told his disciples to be "as shrewd as snakes and as innocent as doves" (Matthew 10:16).

We need to take the same advice in our difficult relationships. We can be innocent because we don't take revenge to hurt others or slander them in our conversations. We'll tell only those who need to know and can help us take steps forward. But we'll be shrewd by not being too vulnerable too soon—not unless or until the person proves to be trustworthy.

Trust isn't established in a moment or a day. It is built brick by brick with respectful, honorable actions—not just words—so that we can be convinced the change is genuine. Some of us make the mistake of believing too quickly. We want the tension to be over and gone, so we overlook inconsistencies and believe the person's words without seeing genuine, long-lasting change. In these cases, the offender often goes back to the same hurtful behavior.

Others of us are too slow to trust. We've been hurt so badly and experienced so little healing that we simply can't trust another person even when he has proven himself time and time again. Trust must be earned, but we need to be willing to give people a chance to win our trust again.

What about you? Do you tend to trust too quickly or too slowly? How have you seen this affect your relationships?

Read Matthew 10:16. If you've experienced a broken or strained relationship, what does it mean for you to be "as shrewd as snakes and as innocent as doves"?

Who do you know who has experienced a restored relationship based on forgiveness and rebuilt trust? What process did those people go through?

Take a moment to read each one of these verses and think about how they apply to your life. Wherever you can do it, insert your name in the verses. Pray these passages over your heart.

- "If it is possible, as far as it depends on you, live at peace with everyone" (Romans 12:18).
- "Bear with each other and forgive one another if any of you has a grievance against someone. Forgive as the Lord forgave you" (Colossians 3:13).

Heart to Heart

One of the most wonderful things I see in women's lives is the beauty of restored relationships. Sometimes, though, women experience God's healing, but their spouse, parents, siblings, or friends refuse to repent for their part in the problem, so trust can't be rebuilt.

Trust involves trusting *and* being trustworthy. We can't control others' choices, but we can do our part to forgive and offer a pathway of restoration for the relationship. This sets us free from the past, even if the other person isn't willing to begin the journey of rebuilding trust.

Matthew 18 challenges us to take the initiative to go to the other person if we've been hurt, rather than waiting for them to 'fess up. Is there anyone in your life right now that you need to forgive...or ask forgiveness of?

⌒

*Lord, give me wisdom to know the difference between
forgiving and excusing. Make me innocent as a dove; wise as
a serpent. I need your wisdom as I seek restoration in my life.*

Week 5

Extraordinary Me:
Searching for Approval and Significance

[identity:] everything about me that makes me who I am, including my unique personality, interests, and life experiences

Some people feel comfortable in their skin, but many of us feel we have to wear masks to cover up who we really are. These masks convey to people that we're fine when we're actually dying inside; that we're calm and relaxed when we're about to explode; that we're confident when we're afraid to reveal how scared we really are.

This week we're going to read the story of Queen Esther, who chose to find her identity in God rather than living in fear of other people and their judgments. We'll also look at Euodia and Syntyche in Philippians, who will be forever remembered for their catty, negative attitudes.

How we think and feel about ourselves determines how we respond to God, to those we love, to opportunities, and to problems. How we think and feel about ourselves determines our attitudes. Rather than searching for everyone's approval, we can live in freedom to become the women God wants us to be.

Zep 3:17

Day 1

A Surprising Role

Be what you are.
This is the first step toward becoming better than you are.
JULIUS CHARLES HARE

Queen of Persia. I'm sure, as a little girl, Esther never imagined the possibility for her life. But, in God's divine plan, he brought an ordinary Jewish woman in exile to a position of power and influence. Esther was faced with some pretty tough decisions: Would she take the safe route and stay silent? Or step out and risk her life for her people? Because Esther's identity was grounded in God, not the king, she was able to take a stand.

In the Word

Read Esther 4 today and pay special attention to verses 13-14:

> *[Mordecai] sent back this answer: "Do not think that because you are in the king's house you alone of all the Jews will escape. For if you remain silent at this time, relief and deliverance for the Jews will arise from another place, but you and your father's family will perish. And who knows but that you have come to your royal position for such a time as this?"*

Esther probably didn't see herself as a heroine. Through some odd circumstances, this beautiful young Jewish woman found herself the Queen of Persia. I'm sure she was dazzled by all the glamour of her position. That was enough for her to think about, but God had other plans.

Haman was one of the king's nobles, but he despised the Jews and plotted to kill them all. At that critical moment in the history of God's people, Esther's cousin Mordecai realized that God had put her in the strategic position as the queen to rescue their people. Mordecai asked her to risk her life by going to the king without being invited so she could ask him to change his edict and save the Jews.

I'm sure Esther was afraid, but she chose to obey God. After fasting for three days, she went to the king to beg for mercy for the Jews. And at the second of two lavish banquets, she exposed Haman's evil plot and rescued her people. This is great stuff, right? Talk about a woman of courage and faith.

All along, Esther had a choice: to enjoy the wealth and prestige of her new position as queen or to realize that God had a surprising role for her. She chose wisely and boldly, risking her life to save her people. Yes, God had orchestrated all of this, but Esther was willing to step up and follow this role that was designed for her. We can be this kind of woman!

Make It Real

Our identity and faith integrity isn't created in a vacuum. It is forged in the fires of difficulties. In these painful and threatening times, we make choices that reveal our true character and shape our futures. Can you think of a time in your life like this?

All of us have made good and bad choices in critical moments. When we lean toward poor discernment or bad decisions, God offers grace and forgiveness. And if we've been hurt in the past, we can respond now with faith and courage to create a new future. I know it can happen. I've seen countless women who have experienced abuse or abandonment, but instead of hiding in shame or becoming bitter, they trusted God to use everything in their lives to create something new and beautiful.

Thomas Merton wrote about the importance of capturing the moment, just as Esther did when she faced her choice:

> The individual person is responsible for living his own life
> and for "finding himself." If he persists in shifting this

responsibility to somebody else, he fails to find out the meaning of his own existence.[1]

Reread Esther 4:1-17. Describe the risk Mordecai asked Esther to take. How would you have felt if you had been Esther?

How have you seen a woman's identity shaped, positively or negatively, by her response in a difficult moment?

If our identity is often forged in the fires of difficulties, what have some of the "fires" been in your life? How have you responded?

Take a moment to read each one of these verses and think about how they apply to your life. Wherever you can do it, insert your name in the verses. Pray these passages over your heart.

- "You have searched me, LORD, and you know me. You know when I sit and when I rise; you perceive my thoughts from afar. You discern my going out and my lying down; you are familiar with all my ways" (Psalm 139:1-3).

- "He who began a good work in you will carry it on to completion until the day of Christ Jesus" (Philippians 1:6).

- "All the days ordained for me were written in your book before one of them came to be" (Psalm 139:16).

Heart to Heart

Who am I? We've all asked the question. Famed psychologist Erik Erikson said that establishing a strong, clear sense of identity is a critical part of life.[2] In this process we have to learn who to trust and who not to trust. We need to figure out what we do well and grasp the scope of our responsibilities. Then we'll be ready to move forward with joy, strength, and confidence in who God created us to be. If we don't take time to develop our identity, we'll constantly be second-guessing ourselves and be insecure in all of our relationships.

Who are *you?* Take a few moments today to ponder and pray about the answer to that important question. Remember, the real you isn't defined just by what you do. It's defined by God, who uniquely hand-crafted you as his daughter.

⌒

Lord, open my eyes to who you created me to be. Thank you for making me "me." Forgive me for sometimes trying to be somebody else. Give me confidence in who you created me to be and help me to take a stand in my life for what's right and true!

Day 2

A Good Reputation

Conduct yourselves in a manner worthy of the gospel.

PHILIPPIANS 1:27

When people think about you, what words come to their minds? I'm not saying we should live as people-pleasers, but God's Word does tell us that we represent Christ, wherever we go and whatever we do. In Philippians, Paul confronts two women who couldn't seem to get along, Euodia and Syntyche. I can definitely identify with their struggle. Arguments happen, but an extraordinary woman strives to act with patience and humility, even when she is frustrated and hurt.

In the Word

Read Philippians 4 today and pay special attention to verses 2-3:

> *I plead with Euodia and I plead with Syntyche to be of the same mind in the Lord. Yes, and I ask you, my true companion, help these women since they have contended at my side in the cause of the gospel, along with Clement and the rest of my co-workers, whose names are in the book of life.*

How would you like to have your name written down in history—in the Bible, no less!—as a complainer? Paul doesn't tell us the cause of the disagreement between these two women, but it was serious enough for him to write it in his letter and have it read publicly. It must have been quite a rift!

How many of us are known in some circles as whiners, complainers, clingy, needy, or some other adjective that isn't exactly one we wanted someone to write in our high school yearbook? Our reputation is our public identity, and we need to be very honest with ourselves about how we're perceived by others.

Our impact for God depends in part on how we are viewed. If others respect and trust us, they'll be eager to listen and let us speak into their lives. However, if they see us as chronically negative, they won't heed our input; they may even avoid being around us.

It doesn't have to be that way. No matter what heartaches and inconveniences we've experienced, we have a God-given opportunity each moment of each day to choose our response. I'm not suggesting that we lie about the pain we feel or the disappointments we've endured, but we can reframe and respond to those hurts with faith and courage. In the same letter, Paul tells the believers at Philippi to soak up the love, tenderness, and grace of Christ so much that those qualities overflow in relationships with others. Here's what he wrote in Philippians 2:1-3:

> If you have any encouragement from being united with Christ, if any comfort from his love, if any common sharing in the Spirit, if any tenderness and compassion, then make my joy complete by being like-minded, having the same love, being one in spirit and of one mind. Do nothing out of selfish ambition or vain conceit. Rather, in humility value others above yourselves.

Make It Real

Being authentic doesn't mean we "let it all hang out" and say everything we feel like saying. That may be our culture's version of being real, but ours is a bit different. We are to be completely honest with God about how we feel, how we see things. We learn to quickly and thoroughly filter every event in our lives through the grace, wisdom, and power of God. It's called "judicious editing." With hearts of renewed love, minds with fresh wisdom, and hands of energized compassion, we choose to trust God to turn every moment of every day into something beautiful.

Read 2 Corinthians 2:14-16. This passage describes our relationships as a pleasing aroma...quite the opposite from what we see with Euodia and Syntyche!

Do you know some women who are "the pleasing aroma of Christ" wherever they go? Name a couple. In what way do they show forth Christ?

Take a look at today's passage again: Philippians 4:1-4. How do you think those ladies felt when this was read about them in their church? How would you have felt?

To what extent is a woman's reputation her real identity?

Read Philippians 2:1-6, 12-18. What would it look like for you to treat other people in this way? How can you be the aroma of Jesus today to the people you meet?

Take a moment to read each one of these verses and think about how they apply to your life. Wherever you can do it, insert your name in the verses. Pray these passages over your heart.

- "A good name is more desirable than great riches; to be esteemed is better than silver or gold" (Proverbs 22:1).

- "Be completely humble and gentle; be patient, bearing with one another in love...Do not let any unwholesome talk come out of your mouths, but only what is helpful for building others up according to their needs" (Ephesians 4:2,29).

- "The name of the righteous is used in blessings, but the name of the wicked will rot" (Proverbs 10:7).

Heart to Heart

Sometimes when I walk out of a conversation or when I leave a group of friends I wonder, *How am I thought of?* I want to bear with my husband, my kids, my friends in love. To live above reproach. To genuinely care about other people, not just what they can do for me.

Heart change doesn't come by gritting our teeth and willing it to happen. Certainly, discipline and determination are important, but we also have to tap into the deep well of God's love and strength so that it flows into us and through us. Catherine Booth is a beautiful example of this. She and her husband William founded The Salvation Army. In serving the poor, she learned that people need more than mere words. She wrote,

> The Gospel…represents Jesus Christ, not as a system of truth to be received into the mind like I should receive a system of philosophy, or astronomy, but it represents Him as a real, living, mighty Saviour, able to save me *now*.[1]

This kind of relationship with Jesus transforms us…one day, one conversation, one moment at a time!

Lord, I know that a good name is more desirable than great riches. Help others to see you in me. Give me wisdom to see the influence I have and the consequences of my behavior.

Day 3

God's Woman

Grace means God's love in action toward people…
who could not lift a finger to save themselves.

J. I. PACKER

At some point in her life, every woman struggles to believe God loves her. She can embrace the truth that God loves the *world*. But she can't fathom God loves *her*. I've had those doubts. When I look at the real me that nobody else sees, my first thought is *how could God love that?*

In his letter to the Ephesians, Paul describes God's crazy, radical love and desire to adopt us as his children. That makes you—and me—God's woman. God's beloved woman.

In the Word

Read Ephesians 1 today and pay special attention to verses 4-8:

> *In love he predestined us for adoption to sonship through Jesus Christ, in accordance with his pleasure and will—to the praise of his glorious grace, which he has freely given us in the One he loves. In him we have redemption through his blood, the forgiveness of sins, in accordance with the riches of God's grace that he lavished on us.*

Grace is a very rare commodity in this world, and unconditional love is scarce. When we read about God's magnificent love for us, offered with no strings attached, it seems too good to be true. But it is true. God's love for you and me is not based on what we do or don't do. In fact, it has nothing at all to do with our performance. God's love for us drove him to the cross, while we were dead in our sin. When we were most unlovable, God chose to love us. Why? "In accordance with his pleasure and will—to the praise of his glorious grace."

In every aspect of life, people are measured by their beauty, brains, and bucks. We hire people because they have skills and experience, and we choose friends because they make us feel good about life. In this passage, Paul goes to great lengths to convince us that God doesn't operate that way at all: He loves us and accepts us as his dearly beloved children *in spite of the fact* that we don't deserve it.

Are you tired of trying to measure up to some arbitrary standard to be acceptable? To be "good enough?" Quit trying. God's incredible grace sets us free. Have you lived with a nagging fear that if people knew your deepest, darkest secrets, they'd reject you? Relax. God knows absolutely everything about you, and he loves you anyway. The measure of God's grace is that he's never surprised by anything we think, say, or do, and he still calls us his own.

Make It Real

For many women, it's tough to grasp the reality of God's grace because we've lived on a performance treadmill all our lives, trying to please enough people and win enough applause to be accepted. Secretly, some of us have concluded that God may *tolerate* us, but he certainly doesn't really *love* us. Paul wants to be sure we get it right. Look at the words he uses to describe our identity as God's dear children. (I know you've read them before, but stop and ponder. Revel in the wonder of what God is actually saying here!)

He adopted us as his children. He is God, and he could have made us slaves, or robots, or rabbits for that matter, but he adopted us into his own family. We're safe and secure in his love.

All of our sins have been forgiven. Paul makes it crystal clear that Christ's death on the cross is the payment for every sin we've ever committed and all those we'll commit in the future. Nothing we've done puts us beyond his mercy and love.

God's love and grace are poured out on us in abundance. Notice the language Paul uses to describe the extent of God's love for us: it is "freely given," it's full of "riches," and he "lavished" it on us. God didn't use a cotton swab to dab his grace on us. Grace is a waterfall that just keeps on flowing. Like a fire hose that destroys our bondage to performance. Like a well of cool, refreshing water that doesn't have any bottom. It can never run out!

Why does God love you?

Read Ephesians 1:3-14 and paraphrase this passage. Which words stand out to you?

What are some ways we measure people's value and acceptance?

How would it (or how does it) affect your sense of identity (confidence, love, compassion, and strength) if you were convinced that God loves you and accepts you unconditionally?

Take a moment to read each one of these verses and think about how they apply to your life. Wherever you can do it, insert your name in the verses. Pray these passages over your heart.

- "Praise be to the God and Father of our Lord Jesus Christ! In his great mercy he has given us new birth into a living hope through the resurrection of Jesus Christ from the dead, and into an inheritance that can never perish, spoil or fade. The inheritance is kept in heaven for you" (1 Peter 1:3-4).

- "But you are a chosen people, a royal priesthood, a holy
  nation, God's special possession, that you may declare
  the praises of him who called you out of darkness into his
  wonderful light" (1 Peter 2:9).

Heart to Heart

God's grace is rich, strong, and real, so why do we have such a
hard time actually living in it? There may be many reasons. Maybe the
people who should have loved you did just the opposite. Maybe you're
afraid to admit that you're flawed, and that you need grace. Perhaps
you feel like your sin is unforgivable. Or you're trying so hard to earn
grace that you've forgotten what grace is—a gift!

Whatever your reason is, know this: Your identity is based on your
conception of grace. As we grasp this transforming truth we'll be free
to be honest about our selfishness and embrace our weakness. We'll be
overcome with God's love for us *in spite of* what we've done. Blaise Pascal wisely observed, "Not only do we not know God except through
Jesus Christ, but also we do not know ourselves except through Jesus
Christ."[1] Ponder that today, and let it soak into your soul.

*God, sometimes I get stuck on the performance treadmill, and
I just want to live as your woman. Free. Alive. Rejoicing in
who you created me to be. Show me how to do that today.*

Day 4

Making a Difference

I am only one, but I am still one. I cannot do everything,
but I can do something. The something I ought to
do, I can do. And by the grace of God, I will.

EDWARD EVERETT HALE

You are who you spend time with. In Luke 10:41-42, the Lord told Martha, "Martha, Martha…you are worried and upset about many things, but few things are needed—or indeed only one. Mary has chosen what is better." Now get this picture in your mind: Martha, scurrying around the house—cooking, cleaning, getting everything ready for her guests. Mary, sitting calmly at Jesus' feet. Listening to his every word.

Sometimes, I feel like Martha. "Julie, Julie…" the Lord says to me as I rush through my day. Ever been there? What is that *one thing* that Jesus spoke of? Being with him. Sitting. Listening. Resting. In today's passage, we'll discover what it means to serve others out of a heart like Mary's.

In the Word

Read Ephesians 2 today and pay special attention to verse 10:

For we are God's handiwork, created in Christ Jesus to do good works, which God prepared in advance for us to do.

As we follow Jesus, we gradually absorb his values and his heart for people. Slowly, he transforms our hearts so that we care about the things he cares about: the lost, the hurting, the old, and the young. We realized that we're his now: We're not our own; we've been bought with a price. As his children, he has given us the unspeakable privilege of making a difference in the lives of those around us.

We aren't on earth to sit, soak, and sour. God wants to use us as his hands to touch people, his feet to meet them where they live, and his mouth to speak words of grace and truth wherever we go. Sometimes, though, you and I became a slave of *doing*...like Martha. We can't say no. We can't stop adding to our plates. We're caught in a crazy schedule of serving, and we rarely stop to be with Jesus. This kind of lifestyle robs our souls of nourishment, and leads to burnout.

On the other hand, some of us indulge ourselves in every possible pleasure that money can buy. We're addicted to the cult of the next thing. But selfish pursuits always leave us wanting more because, sooner or later, they make us feel even emptier. This extreme isn't right either, and it definitely wasn't Mary's attitude. Her heart to serve was an overflow of being with Jesus.

I've known hundreds of women who delight in being used by God to touch a life—often in a small way with a smile, a half hour of time, or an encouraging word, but sometimes with bold visions of changing families and communities. I want to live that way, don't you?

Make It Real

Are you up for God using you in big and small ways? Paul tells us that God has equipped us for that purpose. It's crazy to think how God intricately orchestrates the intersection of others' needs and our abilities to shape their lives. It's not an accident—it's God's divine design. Have you seen this happen in your life?

In his loving sovereignty, God uses our experiences to equip us and help us connect with others who are going through situations similar to ours. Often, God uses the pain of our past to give us compassion for hurting people around us and sharpen our skills to help them. Our past hurts can be the platform for our most fruitful ministry—if we'll trust God to heal us and use us.

You can't do everything. You are one person living in a world full of hurting, needy people. That's hard to accept, sometimes...especially when our hearts ache for other people. But that's where we desperately need God's wisdom to know when to say "yes" and when to say "no." And where do we get that wisdom? From sitting at Jesus' feet, just like Mary did.

God put each of us together uniquely. The New Testament gives us four different lists of spiritual gifts that God uses to equip each of us for specific areas of service. Take a look at 1 Corinthians 12, Romans 12, Ephesians 4, and 1 Peter 4. Some of us are servants. Some of us move hearts by speaking God's Word. And some of us can organize a great event.

If you don't know what your spiritual gifts are, look for places where God seems to be using you already to change lives. Evaluate your life for areas where you sense God's pleasure and power as you serve.

Read Matthew 20:28. How does Jesus' example of selfless service inspire you?

Where have you seen God use you most effectively to change lives, such as organizing meetings, teaching the Word, leading people, etc? How would your best friends answer this question about you?

Reread Ephesians 2:8-10. What's the connection between God's grace and our glad service? What's the connection in your life right now?

Are you more like Martha or Mary? If you're like Martha, how can you spend time at Jesus' feet, rather than just work for him? If you're like Mary, how can you put your faith into action today?

Take a moment to read each one of these verses and think about how they apply to your life. Wherever you can do it, insert your name in the verses. Pray these passages over your heart.

- "The greatest among you will be your servant" (Matthew 23:11).

- "Never be lacking in zeal, but keep your spiritual fervor, serving the Lord" (Romans 12:11).

- "Faith by itself, if it is not accompanied by action, is dead" (James 2:17).

Heart to Heart

Some of us (myself included) can get so busy serving that we're on the edge of burnout. We lose our delight in being with God, just like Martha. If you're doing too much, stop. Redirect your focus and bask in God's love for you. If you're still frazzled, take a break for a while to recharge and regroup. (And don't feel guilty! Rest is biblical.) When you're ready, you can come back with passion and energy, rather than living in survival mode.

Don't worry, God's work isn't completely dependent on you, and in fact, God may tap some other women on the shoulder to serve while you're taking a break. God's task of reaching the world and caring for all the hurting is far from done, but if you try to serve in your own energy, you won't get far. Begin today (and every day) sitting at Jesus' feet, so you can gain his perspective and know where to invest your time and energy to make a difference in your world.

Lord, give me wisdom to know when to serve, and when to say "no" and just sit at your feet. Thank you for the privilege of being used by you today…

Day 5

God Delights in You

The king is enthralled by your beauty;
honor him, for he is your lord.

PSALM 45:11

Y*ou are the King's daughter.* Stop and ponder that. Your heart is all glorious within. You are clothed with righteous robes, interwoven with gold. And none of this is from yourself. It is undeserved and unmerited favor—God's grace.

Wow. When Isaiah started to "get" this, he erupted in praise: "I delight greatly in the LORD; my soul rejoices in my God. For he has clothed me with garments of salvation and arrayed me in a robe of his righteousness...as a bride adorns herself with her jewels" (Isaiah 61:10).

What does it mean to delight in God...and for God to delight in you? Today, we'll find out.

In the Word

Read Romans 12 today and pay special attention to verse 3:

> *For by the grace given me I say to every one of you: Do not think of yourself more highly than you ought, but rather think of yourself with sober judgment, in accordance with the measure of faith God has given you.*

I believe God wants us to have a Goldilocks identity: Not too high, not too low...but just right. Throughout the Bible, God tells us the truth about who we really are. Why does he have to say it so many different ways and so often? Because it's so easy for us to believe the lies of this world and end up on one extreme or the other.

Some of us are pretty self-absorbed. *Look at me, world!* we think. These ladies only talk about themselves, and to be honest, they don't know why anyone would want to talk about anything else! Ever met her?

A whole lot of us, though, find ourselves on the other end of the spectrum: We are plagued with a nagging sense of shame, and we secretly feel worthless, hopeless, and helpless. We try hard to convince people that we're confident and competent. How can we possibly do this when we don't believe it ourselves?

Paul tells us not to think more highly of ourselves than we should. Whatever end of the spectrum you land on, when you and I fail to live out of our true identity in Christ, it can be spiritually devastating. Over and over again, God reminds us in Scripture that we are dearly beloved daughters of the King. Our adoption by God is an inspiring truth that overcomes our sense of worthlessness and shame.

So what does it mean to have a "just right" sense of identity? We are complex creatures. As long as we live on this earth, we war within ourselves: prone to sin, and yet wanting to please God. Both desires exist in us at the same time, and we are wise to acknowledge this fact. I read a statement that summarizes this "just right" identity. It says:

"We are wonderfully created, tragically fallen, deeply loved, and completely forgiven."[1]

Make It Real

Those of us who are self-absorbed need to realize that we are flawed—just like everyone else—and we're just as much in need of God's grace and mercy. Instead of pride and contempt for others, we need to humbly admit that we need God's forgiveness and love.

And those of us who live with a debilitating sense of shame can focus our hearts and minds on the truths of Scripture. As we discover who we are in Christ, and begin to see ourselves through God's eyes, we'll experience the freedom that comes with basing our identity and worth on God's unchanging truth, not how we *feel* in the moment or how we *fail* on a daily basis.

Accepting ourselves is, I believe, impossible until and unless we experience God's acceptance of us by his grace. We didn't earn grace by being good or smart or beautiful, so we can't forfeit it by doing something so bad that he can't forgive us. That's freeing!

How would you describe a "Goldilocks identity"?

If 0 is "self-absorbed" and 10 is "abject shame," where would you put yourself? Why?

Reread Romans 12:1-3. What is the role of faith in establishing your identity in Christ? What do you need to believe God for today in order to find the "extraordinary you"?

Take a moment to read each one of these verses and think about how they apply to your life. Wherever you can do it, insert your name in the verses. Pray these passages over your heart.

- "What a wretched man I am! Who will rescue me from this body of death? Thanks be to God—through Jesus Christ our Lord!" (Romans 7:24-25).

- "Because you are his sons, God sent the Spirit of his Son into our hearts, the Spirit who calls out, '*Abba*, Father.' So you are no longer a slave, but God's child; and since you are his child, God has made you also an heir" (Galatians 4:6-7).

- "The Lord your God is with you, the Mighty Warrior who saves. He will take great delight in you, in his love he will no longer rebuke you, but will rejoice over you with singing" (Zephaniah 3:17).

Heart to Heart

Have you ever gotten tired of all the craziness…the idea that you've got to be perfect, put together, and dance to make everybody happy? Throw in one of those bad hair days. Nothing fits right, nothing looks right, and nothing goes right. You look in the mirror and sigh. Then you hear a little voice from the kitchen that says, "Hey Mom, where's my breakfast?" And it's sure not God talking. This is how days begin for many of us.

If you've had one of those days lately, you probably laughed when you read the title *Becoming a Woman of Extraordinary Faith*. Because you feel pretty average. But the truth is this: What makes you and me extraordinary is not what we *do or don't do*, but the fact that we are loved by an extraordinary God. John 3:16 says, "For God so loved the world that he gave his one and only son." For you. For me. That makes us special.

The woman of extraordinary faith is the woman who knows she is dearly loved by God. It's refreshing to be able to be completely honest with him because he already knows everything about me—and he is thrilled to call me his own. A daughter of the King.

Lord, thank you for creating me as I am. I want to offer myself to you today as a living sacrifice so that I may find my ultimate identity in you…not in what I do or what other people think of me. I choose today to believe that you are the King and I am your daughter, by grace.

Week 6

Extraordinary Love:
Pursued and Cherished by a Relentless God

[love:] a daily decision that involves passion, intimacy, and commitment

To love and be loved. That's what we are made for. Our souls thrive on love, and our relationships grow in proportion to its depth and breadth. We all need someone who's there for us. Someone who makes us feel safe. Secure. Significant.

It's very painful to be in a relationship with someone who doesn't convey their love in a way that makes you feel *really* loved. Tim and I experienced some of that confusion early on in our marriage. When love hurts, it's easy to feel alone. Uncertain. Even angry. You can begin to wonder if real love even exists.

The Bible says in 1 John 4:8 that "God is love." What's interesting about our spiritual journey is we say we believe God loves us. But virtually every woman I know struggles to believe that God really loves her.

This week, we're going to take a look at the nature of extraordinary love. We'll see how God was in the middle of Rebekah's relationship with Isaac, how Mary, the mother of Jesus, exemplified heartfelt love, and how we can experience deeper, richer love in all of our relationships.

We'll see how the radical, transforming love of God changes lives—even yours and mine.

Day 1

Love...in Every Relationship?

*Dear friends, let us love one another, for love comes
from God. Everyone who loves has been born of
God and knows God...Dear friends, since God so
loved us, we also ought to love one another. No one
has ever seen God; but if we love one another, God
lives in us and his love is made complete in us.*

1 JOHN 4:7,11-12

What's love got to do with it? While Tina Turner belted out this question, many of us sang along. But do we know the answer? Anything? *Everything!* We tend to view love as romance, feeling, passion...but what if "love comes from God"? What does that mean? What would that look like? Rebekah's story is a beautiful example of a woman who trusted God with her love life and invited God into her love story.

In the Word

Read Genesis 24 today and pay special attention to verses 66-67:

*Then the servant told Isaac all he had done. Isaac brought her
into the tent of his mother Sarah, and he married Rebekah. So
she became his wife, and he loved her.*

Have you noticed how we compartmentalize our lives? We have a church life, a family life, a career, hobbies, exercise, and other aspects of life that are strung together like pearls on a necklace. The modern-day tragedy is that we don't invite God into every area of our lives—to be at the center of every activity and every relationship. We need his wisdom, love, and strength all day, every day, not just when we're in church on Sunday morning or in a women's Bible study. The love story of Isaac and Rebekah shows us how they invited God to be in the middle of their relationship, and it made all the difference in the world!

I'm reminded of Psalm 127:1: "Unless the LORD builds the house, the builders labor in vain." God had promised Abraham and Sarah a son, and after many years of waiting (sometimes, impatiently waiting), Isaac was born. When he became a young man and wanted to marry, Abraham wanted him to have a wonderful wife.

So he sent his servant to a distant land to find the right woman for his son. (Sounds like a great plan someday for our kids!) From the beginning of the search, Abraham and his servant prayed for God's direction.

When the servant arrived in Nahor, he asked God to arrange a test of character to show him the woman God had chosen. Without being asked, she would offer to give his camels a drink. Soon, the women of the town appeared at the well, and one of them offered to draw water for the servant's ten camels.

He struck up a conversation, and found that the girl was a distant relative of Abraham's. Her family invited the servant to spend the night with them, and to their astonishment, he explained that God had led him there to ask for Rebekah's hand in marriage for Isaac. She agreed, and the next morning, she packed her camel and left her family for the adventure of marriage.

Make It Real

The particulars of this story probably won't be repeated in any of our lives, but the principle is certainly timeless and transforming: We can invite God to be in the center of every relationship—with our husbands, our children, our parents, our siblings, our friends and neighbors, and the people we work with.

Abraham and his servant trusted God to direct them from the beginning, and the servant asked God for a test of character to reveal the bride God had selected. With the confidence of answered prayer, the servant boldly made his offer of marriage to the stunned young lady and her family. And eventually, when Isaac met Rebekah, their love was based on the firm foundation of God's leading and God's pleasure in their relationship.

> Reread Genesis 24:34-51. How would you have felt and responded if you had been Rebekah listening to the servant's account of God leading him to ask her to marry Isaac?

> Think of one or two important relationships in your life. What would it mean for you to trust God for direction to build or rebuild these?

> As you trust God in these relationships, what are you responsible to be, say, and do? What is beyond your control?

Take a moment to read each one of these verses and think about how they apply to your life. Wherever you can do it, insert your name in the verses. Pray these passages over your heart.

- "This is how we know what love is: Jesus Christ laid down his life for us. And we ought to lay down our lives for our brothers and sisters" (1 John 3:16).

- "Love is patient, love is kind. It does not envy, it does not boast, it is not proud. It does not dishonor others, it is not self-seeking, it is not easily angered, it keeps no record of wrongs" (1 Corinthians 13:4-5).

- "There is no fear in love. But perfect love drives out fear, because fear has to do with punishment. The one who fears is not made perfect in love. We love because he first loved us" (1 John 4:18-19).

Heart to Heart

As you've read this marvelous story and thought about its implications, maybe your heart is discouraged. Maybe you've given up hoping that the relationships in your life could even be any different. Face it—we've all been there.

Some of us haven't trusted God to lead us in our relationships, and we can't go back and start over. That's okay. God invites us to start right now, right here, with the relationships we have, and he delights for us to ask him to be the center of them all. Even if we've made terrible mistakes in the past—and more pointedly, *because* we've made mistakes in the past—God wants us to trust him to guide us as we build and rebuild the most important relationships of our lives.

What would that look like? Challenging. Thrilling. A little bit scary, even. If we ask him, God will give us courage to face our fears and heartaches, to speak words of forgiveness and hope, and to wisely discern who to trust.

We can't make others respond the way we want them to, but we can trust God to give us grace and peace whether they respond positively or not. Through it all, we can have the enduring sense that we are walking with God as we relate to each person in our lives—whether that's a boss, a friend, a neighbor, or our husband. And that assurance gives us confidence and hope.

No matter what condition your relationships are in right now, invite God to be in the middle of them all.

⌒

Father, some of my relationships are not what they should be or all they could be. Show me where I have failed and help me rebuild them. God, I invite you into my relationships. Let your love flow through me and give me wisdom.

Day 2

Heartfelt Love

It is not how much you do,
but how much love you put into the doing that matters.
MOTHER TERESA

How does it feel to stand by and watch your beloved son be brutally murdered? I can't imagine it. For Mary the mother of Jesus, the journey of loving wasn't easy. As a mother, every fiber in Mary's body must have been screaming out, wanting to do anything to protect Jesus, her son, from the torturous death of crucifixion. But since that night many years before, as she lovingly gazed at her newborn son, she'd known he had been born in the shadow of the cross.

In the Word

Read Luke 2 today and pay special attention to verses 16-19:

> So they hurried off and found Mary and Joseph, and the baby, who was lying in the manger. When they had seen him, they spread the word concerning what had been told them about this child, and all who heard it were amazed at what the shepherds said to them. But Mary treasured up all these things and pondered them in her heart.

Sometimes I wonder what it was like for Jesus' mother in those last days, the last hours, and the last moments of his life. Mary's agony must have been excruciating. Yes, she knew Jesus was God's Son and his appointed sacrifice to pay for the sins of all mankind, but it was also *her* beloved son who was suffering and dying!

Mary's courage and love had been tested many times since the angel first announced that she would bear God's Messiah. In response to the angel's incredible message, she sang of her trust in God's sovereignty and goodness. When the baby was born, a host of angels filled the heavens with praises, and humble shepherds reported the news of the angelic concert to the young parents.

Luke tells us that Mary "treasured" these things up and "pondered them in her heart." She absorbed the meaning of every moment because she realized she had a pivotal role to play.

Make It Real

We can make one of two mistakes in loving relationships: isolation or enmeshment. In isolation, we withhold our commitment to care, to be involved, and to take responsibility. Perhaps we've been hurt too many times or emotionally damaged so severely that we don't know how to connect with people. We may be in the same room with people and engage in conversations with them, but our connections remain shallow and distant and never deepen.

The opposite error is to lose ourselves in relationships, to devote all our energies to controlling others' attitudes, words, beliefs, and behaviors. In doing that, we let them control us. We may call it love but it's mutual manipulation, and it eventually drives people away. Stop and think about it. In your relationships, do you tend more toward isolation or enmeshment?

Mary's love was the epitome of *non-possessive warmth*, genuine affection that desires the best for another person without demanding or controlling. She could have felt the crushing responsibility to control Jesus when he was a boy, but she neither withdrew in fear nor compulsively fixed his every problem. She entrusted him to God, loved him with all her heart, and let him grow in responsibility as an adult. (The writer to the Hebrews says that Jesus "learned obedience from what he suffered"...not fun as a mom!) Throughout the accounts in the Scriptures, we see Mary's heartfelt love for Jesus, knowing that the Father's will for him was far more important than her motherly desires for his peace and protection.

How would you define and describe authentic love, isolation, and enmeshment?

Read over Luke 1:38, Luke 1:54, Luke 2:16-19, and John 19:25-27. How do you think "treasuring" insights and "pondering" their implications helped Mary continue to love Jesus without withdrawing or controlling him?

Consider one person you love. What does it (or would it) mean for you to love this person with Mary's kind of heartfelt love?

Take a moment to read each one of these verses and think about how they apply to your life. Wherever you can do it, insert your name in the verses. Pray these passages over your heart.

- "This is love: not that we loved God, but that he loved us and sent his Son as an atoning sacrifice for our sins. Dear friends, since God so loved us, we also ought to love one another. No one has ever seen God; but if we love one another, God lives in us and his love is made complete in us" (1 John 4:10-12).
- "A new command I give you: Love one another. As I have loved you, so you must love one another. By this everyone will know that you are my disciples, if you love one another" (John 13:34-35).

Heart to Heart

Mary is a wonderful example of how to serve in the important relationships in my life. I'm not raising the Son of God, and I'm certainly not Mary; but I can model her perspective, desires, and actions. I can treasure the times God gives me a glimpse of his heart for those I love, and I can ponder how to partner with God in their lives instead of getting in the way by controlling them.

True sacrificial love means that I care more about God's purposes for the people in my life than my own dreams for them. Is it hard? Sure! But perhaps my first task is to ask God to help me align my dreams for them with his. Until that happens, I'll be fighting against him, or at least confused about my role in their lives. But this alignment is only the first step.

Mary might have wanted to get out of her role as she saw the Father's will unfold day after day in Jesus' life. On the way to the cross, he was ridiculed and mocked by his enemies, and misunderstood by his closest friends. But Mary's devotion to God's plan for Jesus never wavered.

Have you ever wrestled with overcontrolling, overprotecting, or overencouraging those you love? As women, what do you think drives us to act this way? Ask God for wisdom today to love the people in your life in a way that frees them up to become all that God wants them to be.

God, your sacrificial love for me astounds me. Thank you! Show me how to love other people in the way you have loved me—unconditionally, sacrificially, with all of my heart.

Day 3

Embracing the Mystery

To lose mystery is to lose wonder, reverence,
and worship. A God that can be fully explained
is hardly a God worth worshipping!
RICHARD VINCENT

When I try to comprehend the love of God for me, it literally boggles my mind. As women, many of us struggle with feeling unloved, insecure, and "less-than." When our emotions drop, we forget that once and for all, Jesus has proved his love for us on the cross. You and I were spiritually dead, justly deserving God's judgment, and Jesus, in love, took our sin upon himself. Every sin that separates you and me from God has been paid for and forgiven! And more than that, Jesus pursues our hearts, wooing us with his love. Have you stopped to look for his love-gifts to you today?

In the Word

Read John 17 today and pay special attention to verses 22-23:

> *[Jesus prayed,] "I have given them the glory that you gave me, that they may be one as we are one—I in them and you in me—so that they may be brought to complete unity. Then the world will know that you sent me and have loved them even as you have loved me."*

We read about it, we sing about it, and we hear messages about it, but we can never seem to grasp the full extent of God's magnificent love for us. In beautiful, poetic language, Paul prayed for the Ephesians, that they would "get" God's love:

> And I pray that you, being rooted and established in love, may have power, together with all the Lord's holy people, to grasp how wide and long and high and deep is the love of Christ, and to know this love that surpasses knowledge— that you may be filled to the measure of all the fullness of God (Ephesians 3:17-19).

Is it possible to *know* something that's beyond knowledge, or is that just "preacher-speak"? Throughout the Bible, we see remarkable accounts of God's love for those who are unlovely, his patient kindness for those who seldom love him in return, and his desire to shower good on those who ignore him. His love is truly amazing!

We can read about and study aspects of God's love, but paradoxically, the more we grasp his love, the more we realize it is beyond our comprehension. That's what Paul is talking about. God's love isn't just sentimental warmth that fades when life gets dark. No, we see the extent of his radiant love when Jesus endured great suffering and ridicule so that he could pour his life out for people—even the ones who didn't understand or accept it.

In his prayer the night he was betrayed, Jesus said some remarkable things to the Father. He asked that God would overwhelm us with his love and power, his tenderness and majesty, so that our lives would be truly transformed.

In other words, if we taste of God's love, we'll never be the same. And Jesus makes another astounding request: He asks that our love for God and for each other would be so great that the world would recognize that God loves every person on the earth as much as the Father loves the Son!

Make It Real

The mystery of the Trinity—the unity of the Father, Son, and Spirit—amazes us and often confounds us, but exploring it gives us a glimpse of the measure of God's abundant love for us.

Author and speaker Larry Crabb wrote:

> Mystery can neither be mastered nor managed. But mystery can be entered—first with the heart, then in limited, but deep and exciting, ways with the head. More often than not, we're drawn to belief through the door of desire.[1]

Do you desire to know the unknowable depths of God's love? To reach its unreachable heights, and, when you've been overwhelmed by it, to realize you've only taken the first steps in your understanding of it? I do.

Crabb advises us to "get lost in the trinity. Wonder before its sheer delight and inexplicability. Let yourself be drawn into its transcendent and compelling appeal."[2]

What are some things you can do to increase your sense of wonder at the goodness and greatness of God?

Read Ephesians 3:14-21. What do you think it means "to know this love that surpasses knowledge"?

Stop to ponder the love of the Trinity. How does it affect you to realize that the Father loves you as much as he loves the Son?

Take a moment to read each one of these verses and think about how they apply to your life. Wherever you can do it, insert your name in the verses. Pray these passages over your heart.

- "But God demonstrates his own love for us in this: While we were still sinners, Christ died for us" (Romans 5:8).

- "And over all these virtues put on love, which binds them all together in perfect unity" (Colossians 3:14).
- "Greater love has no one than this, that he lay down his life for his friends" (John 15:13).

Heart to Heart

Because we live in a very scientific, technological age, we expect or are expected to know how things work, from iPhone apps to relationships. Sure, we've gained a lot in this pursuit, but we've lost something precious: a sense of wonder.

There are plenty of things that we can learn with practical measures: ten simple steps to start it, eight steps to fix it, four steps to maintain it. *But some aspects of life simply can't be reduced to formulas.* The love of God is at the top of that list.

Contemplating the relationships of the Father, Son, and Spirit in the Trinity may make our brains hurt, and we certainly won't end up with a neat, simple answer to the mystery. But the pursuit is the reward. Exploring God's nature expands our minds, fills our hearts, and eventually, changes how we respond to every person and situation in our lives. It's worth the effort.

Today, embrace the mystery of the Trinity. And ponder that love... the same love with which God loves you!

Lord, my heart is filled with sacred discontent. I need you more, and I know that. I want to know and experience your love, like never before. Open the eyes of my heart. Fill my cup, Lord, until it overflows with you and your love.

Day 4

Loving God

Count every day lost that you have not spent in loving God.
BROTHER LAWRENCE

f you love me, you will obey me," Jesus told his disciples...and us. What does it mean to love God? Surely, it's more than the emotional high we experience at times while singing a worship song. And it's more than the dull, dry reality of following biblical rules. Love is a reality that permeates everything that an extraordinary woman says and does. Love for God drives her, grounds her, frees her, and motivates her.

In the Word

Read Psalm 18 today and pay special attention to verses 1-2:

> *I love you, LORD, my strength.*
> *The LORD is my rock, my fortress and my deliverer;*
> *my God is my rock, in whom I take refuge,*
> *my shield and the horn of my salvation, my stronghold.*

How do we experience love in a relationship with an invisible God, one who is so vast in his power that he spoke a word and billions of galaxies were flung into space? Once, he walked the earth "with skin on" so that people could see him and touch him, but even then, most people didn't understand who he was. Today we have the benefit of hindsight, but we sometimes long for something tangible.

I believe God wants it this way so that we will pursue him with all our hearts and not be constrained by visual images that might limit our faith. Knowing God is a spiritual matter, and God has created our hearts to grasp even more than our minds can imagine. Our love for God is a response to our perception of his love for us.

The more we understand the truth of grace, the more we'll be amazed that God loves us, and our hearts will overflow with appreciation and affection for him. First John 4:19 says it this way: "We love because he first loved us." It's a wonderful truth token that your heavenly Father loves you. When you feel safe in his arms, you are free to love others.

A real danger in our love for God is to believe we deserve more than he has given to us. Somewhere in the core of our being, we believe we've gotten the short end of the stick. We look around and notice a nicer house, a richer husband, and women who have more successful children. And we don't like it one bit!

Our perception (often not articulated, but there just the same) is: I deserve better than this! And that's when things start to get messy.

Make It Real

Entitlement shatters love. Demanding more from God creates a barrier that can't be broken down until one of two things happens: We either get everything we want, or we change our perceptions and our demands melt into thankfulness. Even if our dreams come true and we get everything we demand, we're only satisfied for a short while, and then we expect even more.

This is a great place for a time out. The Bible paints a not-too-glowing picture of our condition apart from Christ. You and I were helpless, hopeless, enemies of God, completely devoted to selfish pursuits, but, at exactly the right time, God reached out of heaven and sent forth his Son to redeem us, to rescue us from sin and death, that we might be adopted as daughters of God. Now that is love.

What does this have to do with expressing love for God? Everything! When our hearts are refreshed with the truth of his grace, we can't help but express our love for him. When we contemplate the fact that he forgave us for our selfish demands, we can't help but thank him.

What are some ways unrealistic expectations and demands erode our love for God?

Reread Psalm 18:1-2. Paraphrase these verses and pray them to the Lord.

Who are some friends who inspire you to love God more? Describe the impact they have on you.

How can you encourage the people around you to love God, too?

Take a moment to read each one of these verses and think about how they apply to your life. Wherever you can do it, insert your name in the verses. Pray these passages over your heart.

- "I have loved you with an everlasting love; I have drawn you with unfailing kindness" (Jeremiah 31:3).
- "But from everlasting to everlasting the LORD's love is with those who fear him" (Psalm 103:17).
- "Love the Lord your God with all your heart and with all your soul and with all your mind and with all your strength" (Mark 12:30).

Heart to Heart

Let's be real. We don't always focus our minds on these truths. I love what missionary Iris Lowder writes,

When you are lonely, you can pray, "Jesus, I belong to you, and I know you're with me whether I feel your presence or not."

When you are afraid, you can pray, "Lord, I belong to you, and I know you understand what's going on even when I don't."

When you are happy, you can pray, "Jesus, I belong to you, and I'm grateful for all you've done for me."

And when you fantasize about escaping to an easier or more exciting life, you can pray, "Lord, I belong to you, and you've chosen for me to walk with you through some difficult times so my faith will grow stronger."

Love begets love. The more we see and experience God, the more we will love him…not just for what he's done for us, but who he is.

God, my love is weak and small, and to be quite honest, I do not know how to love you. Teach me how to love you, Lord. Reveal yourself to me and give me a desire for you.

Day 5

Loving People

You cannot love without giving.

AMY CARMICHAEL

Last words are important. They mark a person's life and leave behind a legacy. Jesus' last words are stunningly simple: *Love one another.* Three simple words, but two thousand years later, we are still grappling with that statement. Our hearts are naturally selfish, but as the Holy Spirit begins to change and transform us, we begin to see people the way God sees them. Rather than judging, criticizing, or belittling, an extraordinary woman begins to love other people not for what *she* can get out of it, but as an overflow of God's love in her heart.

In the Word

Read John 13 today and pay special attention to verses 34-35:

[Jesus told them] "A new command I give you: Love one another. As I have loved you, so you must love one another. By this everyone will know that you are my disciples, if you love one another."

Jesus gave this command to his disciples in the last days before he died. They had traipsed around the country with him for three years, marveling at his power to heal and cast out demons, wondering at his wisdom as he confronted the angry religious establishment, and enjoying a thousand campfire conversations as he demonstrated his love to them every day. These people had a front row seat to see God's love made real! And now, Jesus told them to love each other the same way he had loved them: deliberately, unconditionally, and wisely.

The history of the church tells us that large organizations have often failed miserably to follow Jesus' lead in loving each other, but here and there, individuals and clusters of committed believers have become his hands and feet to love each other. We can't expect organizations to make love a reality in the give and take of daily relationships, but individually, each of us can do our part.

Jesus' command to love each other was not just for the disciples. It is for each of us.

Make It Real

Jesus loved deliberately. He came to pour out his life for us, to serve, not to be served. Love wasn't an addendum he might get to if he had time at the end of his busy day. It was central to everything he said and did. Every relationship, every action, and every word was directed by his love.

In my relationships, I have to ask God for help to show my love for Tim, my children, my friends, and those I serve in Extraordinary Women. Actually, the "plan to love" is often formed as I pray for them and me, and God's Spirit shows me how I sometimes can be an answer to my prayers for them.

Jesus loved unconditionally. I have to laugh—and sometimes I want to cry—when I think of how Jesus poured his heart out to the people who followed him, and they just didn't get it! Day after day, he embodied deity to them, taught them about God's character, and demonstrated God's heart, but when Jesus was arrested, almost all of them ran. For three years, day and night, they witnessed everything. And still they ran. Time after time, Jesus refused to get angry when the disciples were so dense. Day after day, he patiently modeled and instructed them (again) in the ways of God.

I'm so glad and grateful that Jesus is just as patient with us. Sometimes I'm as slow to believe and just as gripped by fear and doubt as they were, but Jesus continues to patiently love me and you. I have people in my life who aren't instantly responsive or cooperative, but when I think about Jesus' patience toward me, I can find more patience for them.

Jesus loved wisely. He wasn't just a sweet guy who never had an unkind word about anyone. He was totally committed to truth, and he wanted people to make revolutionary commitments to follow him. Jesus' love was demonstrated in his tough teaching and his radical devotion to God's will, and he called his followers to lay down their lives, too.

But Jesus always reminded the disciples that if they would lose their lives for his sake, they'd find the abundant life they'd always longed for. Jesus, John tells us, was "full of grace and truth." Most of the people in my life need warmth and affirmation, but they need truth, too. We love people wisely when we blend grace *and* truth into our daily lives.

Read John 13:34-35. What images and teaching do you think came to Jesus' followers' minds as they heard these words?

Describe what you think it means to love people deliberately, unconditionally, and wisely. How can you grow this kind of love in your relationships?

Has anyone come to mind as you've read today's lesson? If so, ask God for specific direction to help love this person.

Take a moment to read each one of these verses and think about how they apply to your life. Wherever you can do it, insert your name in the verses. Pray these passages over your heart.

- "Now that you have purified yourselves by obeying the truth so that you have sincere love for each other, love one another deeply, from the heart" (1 Peter 1:22).

- "Love must be sincere. Hate what is evil; cling to what is good. Be devoted to one another in love. Honor one another above yourselves" (Romans 12:9-10).

- "Make my joy complete by being like-minded, having the same love, being one in spirit and of one mind. Do nothing out of selfish ambition or vain conceit. Rather, in humility value others above yourselves, not looking to your own interests but each of you to the interests of the others" (Philippians 2:2-4).

Heart to Heart

Love is a word we use quite often in our culture, but Jesus' version of it was very different. Love was central to everything Jesus said and did. Every relationship, every action, and every word was directed by his love. That's how I want to live, too.

Far more than just warm, fuzzy feelings, extraordinary love is guided by our heavenly Father's desire for our good, not just our pleasure. This love is inspired to serve rather than demand its own way. It cares so much that it unapologetically calls people to a higher commitment to God.

And that's how you and I can love the people around us.

~

Lord, open my eyes up to see people the way that you see them. Teach me how to love, not judge. Give me compassion and genuine care for the people you've put in my life.

[handwritten notes in top margin:] Gerald Kay — Adam's dad ← — Julie's - ex boyfriend — Jamie's brother — house burned — Alon & Lisa

Extraordinary Dreams:
Free from Disappointment and Regret

*[dreams:] my plans, desires, goals, and
longings about the future*

[handwritten:] Jesus - Just the mention of His name! in Him we have

reams. As a little girl, what did you imagine for your life? What
dreams did you carry in your heart as you first held hands with a
loving guy or walked down the aisle to marry and start a life adventure
with someone? How did the anticipation of a big change, a first baby,
or a new job fill you with anticipation of possibilities? Many of us have
experienced such times of dreaming, but we've also experienced dreams
fading to the background when real life work, effort, trials, and change
become our daily experience.

There are some women who get up every morning with a sense of
destiny, knowing that what they will do that day really matters. Believe
it or not, these women actually exist. They have a spark in their eyes
that tells me they are fully alive. I don't know about you, but I love to
be around them.

Far too many of us settle for something less—far less. Maybe we
had dreams in the past that energized us and motivated us to attempt
great things, but no longer. Now we drift from one activity to another,
only occasionally feeling a jolt of hope that what we're doing really
matters. And when we stop and think about the legacy we're leaving behind, we don't know where to begin and decide that we'll just
start tomorrow. And so we do what's easy. We push any thought of

[handwritten at bottom:] My job is to be obedient - His is to control, 1 Thes 5:24

accomplishing our dreams into our subconscious. We pretend that all is well. But deep down, we know it's not.

This week, we're going to look at two women, Sarah and Anna. God gave both of them a wonderful dream for their lives. In their own ways, they struggled to see the dream fulfilled, but their faith is an example for us as we try to clarify and capture God's dream for us. We'll also look at some other insights about uncovering God's dream for each of us.

I don't have to fear letting God down when I was never responsible for holding Him up.

Satan is the de-motivator. God is stronger than his schemes

The more truth I have in me the less room for lies

Prov 3:5-6

Day 1

Beyond Anything We Can Imagine

Take delight in the LORD, and he will give
you the desires of your heart.

PSALM 37:4

Little girls dream of being princesses. Ballerinas. Superwoman. And then life happens. Lost in the daily grind, we sometimes long for the simple days of childhood and daydreaming. But what if God has more in mind? What if God has dreams for you beyond anything you can imagine? For Sarah, the dream sounded so far-fetched that she laughed.

In the Word

Read Genesis 18 today and pay special attention to verse 12:

> *So Sarah laughed to herself as she thought, "After I am worn out and my lord is old, will I now have this pleasure?"*

You and I probably would have laughed, too. God had promised Abraham and Sarah that they would be the parents of a "great nation," but there were problems: Age and some body parts that weren't working the way they needed to! Abraham and Sarah had no children, and Sarah was far past her childbearing years. In fact, they were old enough to be great-grandparents!

When God first spoke to Abraham and Sarah, I'm sure they were excited. But nothing happened...for years. We can assume they did their part, but Sarah didn't become pregnant. When our dreams aren't fulfilled in the way or the time we expect, we're tempted to move on to Plan B. That's what Sarah did. She decided that she must have misunderstood God's promise, so she sent her maid, Hagar, into Abraham's bedroom, and Hagar bore a son. Ishmael.

Sarah's Plan B, though, wasn't God's dream for her and Abraham. Years later, God sent three angels, disguised as men, to remind them of the original promise. While Sarah was cooking, she overheard their conversation. One of the men told Abraham, "I will surely return to you about this time next year, and Sarah your wife will have a son."

Was Sarah encouraged? Did this strengthen her resolve? No, she laughed! She couldn't imagine God finally coming through with the promise made so long ago, but he did. It's amazing how God works! A year later, Sarah gave birth to little Isaac, whose name means "laughter."

Make It Real

The path of fulfilling God's dreams always includes adventures, delays, disappointments, and fresh enthusiasm. Just ask Sarah. One woman described her dream this way:

> I want to live my life very *purposely*, regularly reviewing and praying over my purpose in life, loving God intensely, cherishing and inspiring my husband, praying for and keeping connected spiritually with my children, loving women and seeking to lay spiritual foundations in their lives.
>
> I want to live *faithfully*, believing God for what I cannot see. I want to believe that God can do in my children's lives what I cannot do.
>
> I want to live *creatively*, creating beauty and warmth in my home, around my table, and in my Bible study. Creativity adds sparkle to a focused, purposeful life.
>
> I want to live *paradoxically*. I want to go against my selfish nature, against our culture, giving a little bit more than I feel like giving, going the second mile, being like Jesus.[1]

Following God's dream for your life will not always make sense.

You may often feel as if God's just forgotten about you. Your feelings of anger, jealousy, fear, and sadness that develop as a result are real. Be honest with God about them. Pretending they're not there will lead to deeper bitterness, coveting, and paralysis. And moving forward with other life goals will seem impossible because you'll likely stay stuck in what *could* have been rather than what *will* be. You'll feel stuck. Bored. Empty. Exhausted. And longing for more.

Trusting God to give you a dream is the first step. Understand that God's dream for you may not be the creation of a new nation to bless the entire planet, but it will be challenging, fulfilling, and it will change the lives of people around you—including your own. The challenge is to embrace it. To pray over it daily. To stay faithful to his promise. To embrace and live out his beauty. To live a holy life, set apart from the rest of the world around you.

Take a few minutes to read about the moment God gave the dream to Abraham and Sarah in Genesis 12:1-5. Write down three dreams you have (or had) for your life that are unfulfilled:

- _____

- _____

- _____

Relate your experience to Sarah's. As the years went by her body aged and no child formed in her womb. How have you responded to unfulfilled dreams? Write it beside each dream above.

Have you hidden any of those feelings under a pretense?

Why is it that you may have been or are afraid to say how you really feel that these dreams have not gone as you had wished?

Have you given up? Are you running away from the dream?

Have you resorted to a plan B, creating your own Ishmael? Something other than what God has? In other words, did you doubt God but pretend you didn't by creating your own plan?

Take a moment to read each one of these verses and think about how they apply to your life. Wherever you can do it, insert your name in the verses. Pray these passages over your heart.

- "Now to him who is able to do immeasurably more than all we ask or imagine, according to his power that is at work within us, to him be glory in the church and in Christ Jesus throughout all generations, for ever and ever! Amen" (Ephesians 3:20-21).

- "And we know that in all things God works for the good of those who love him, who have been called according to his purpose" (Romans 8:28).

Heart to Heart

Sometimes, I get stuck pretending rather than actually pursuing God's dream for me. What about you? Are you pretending in your spiritual walk? You say, "God is good; all the time, God is good." But deep down, you really don't believe it. Maybe it was your divorce. Your parent's divorce. Abuse. Abortion. A miscarriage. The death of a loved one. A hysterectomy. Depression.

And you wonder every day, "God, where are you?" Hear this: God has a dream for you, a purpose for your life. He has always had that dream for you, since before you were born. What would it mean for you to have a clear, compelling dream that captures your heart and propels you to live for something bigger than yourself? How would that change the way you live today? Today, ask God to show you his dreams for you, and give you courage to step out on faith.

—

God, how comforting it is to know that you have plans and dreams for my life! Even when I'm confused, and I'm ready to give up on dreaming, I thank you that you are right here with me.

Day 2

Finally!

The Christian life is not a constant high.
Sometimes, I have to go to God in prayer with tears in
my eyes, and say, "O God, forgive me," or "Help me."
BILLY GRAHAM

Dreams are fragile. They can be eroded by discouragement. Shattered by trauma. Or dreams can simply evaporate because after a while we've forgotten, we've given up hope, we've moved on. Anna didn't let that happen, even after sixty years of waiting at the temple.

In the Word

Read Luke 2 today and pay special attention to verse 38:

> *Coming up to them at that very moment, [Anna] gave thanks*
> *to God and spoke about the child to all who were looking for-*
> *ward to the redemption of Jerusalem.*

Anna was one of the most persistent women in the Bible. She married. Lived with her husband until he died after just seven years of marriage. Imagine the devastation. Dreams of a long life filled with playing, dancing, laughing, and being together with her family—vanished. All gone.

To make matters worse, in those days many girls married when they were 13, so her husband may have died when she was just 20 years old. But Anna was persistent. Committed to a new dream. Until the age of 84, likely for more than 60 years, she stayed in the temple in Jerusalem "night and day" worshipping God.

Imagine trading a life filled with a husband and children—a beautiful family to have fun and grow old with—for a trip into the temple *every day*. It seems like Anna got a bum deal. When life doesn't seem fair, it's easy for us (for me, anyway) to grumble and complain because we didn't get what we're sure we deserved. We look around at others with happy marriages, big bank accounts, wonderful vacations, and perfect kids (or so it seems), and conclude, "God has forgotten about me." Self-pity and discouragement take hold.

Comparison strangles the life out of every one of us—it's an equal opportunity discourager! When we focus on what others have, and we resent the fact that they have more than we have (even if we'd never say it out loud), a cloud of doubt hovers over our lives and shrouds every relationship and activity. Anna refused to let that happen. If there was ever a woman who got a bad deal, it was Anna. She trusted God, but all it got her was a dead husband and decades of loneliness. But that's not how Anna looked at life. Instead, her belief in God led her down a different path. She eagerly anticipated God showing up one day to reveal the promised Messiah.

And that's exactly what happened. When Mary and Joseph took their baby into the temple, Anna was there as she had been for so many years. On that day, her heart had been prepared to capture the dream she had often imagined over so many years. She was sensitive to God's Spirit, and she knew the baby the poor young couple was carrying was the One. Her waiting was over! Luke tells the story, "Coming up to them at that very moment, she gave thanks to God and spoke about the child to all who were looking forward to the redemption of Jerusalem" (Luke 2:38).

Make It Real

I can imagine that every day for all those years, Anna kept reminding herself of the dream God had given her to serve him quietly and faithfully. And that's what it takes. A daily reminder that God is who he says he is. It takes perseverance and focus to start every day in prayer, reminding ourselves that God does not lie (Numbers 23:19; Titus 1:2) but instead has our best interest in mind (Jeremiah 29:11; Psalm 32:10).

It's what God told Moses in Deuteronomy 8:11, "Be careful that you do not forget the LORD your God."

Luke doesn't tell us that God gave Anna a grand promise like he gave Abraham and Sarah. No, Anna's dream was to stay in God's presence and be available for anything he wanted to show her, give her, or direct her to do. She personified Psalm 27:4 *One thing I ask from the LORD, this only do I seek: that I may dwell in the house of the LORD all the days of my life, to gaze on the beauty of the LORD and to seek him in his temple.*

When has comparison inevitably led to self-pity and discouragement for you?

Some of us have stopped dreaming altogether, but as we begin to investigate God's dreams for our lives, we must be careful to tread biblically. What potential dangers do you see in becoming overly focused on finding God's dream?

In addition to perseverance to hold on to God's dream, what qualities can we learn from Anna?

How is the dream of being available and faithful to God every day just as important as dramatic visions?

How can you be available and faithful to God every day? What changes do you need to make in your daily life to be more available?

Take a moment to read each one of these verses and think about how they apply to your life. Wherever you can do it, insert your name in the verses. Pray these passages over your heart.

- "But the plans of the LORD stand firm forever, the purposes of his heart through all generations" (Psalm 33:11).

- "Commit to the LORD whatever you do, and he will establish your plans" (Proverbs 16:3).

- "Stand firm. Let nothing move you. Always give yourselves fully to the work of the Lord, because you know that your labor in the Lord is not in vain" (1 Corinthians 15:58).

Heart to Heart

Dare to dream about how God can use you to impact your neighborhood, community, and church in great ways. God-given dreams aren't about wealth or power. They are about matters of God's heart: helping the hurting, reaching the lost, and providing resources for those in need.

Marian Wright Edelman, the president and founder of the Children's Defense Fund, learned what really matters. She commented, "Never work just for money or for power. They won't save your soul... or help you sleep at night...Service is the rent we pay to be living. It is the very purpose of life and not something you do in your spare time."[1]

If you haven't found something that grips your heart, don't settle. Instead, encounter God by praying and spending time in his presence. When you seek the dream, you'll always come up empty. But when you seek God, you will always find the dream. Anna's faithfulness led her to literally holding the promised Messiah in her arms and proclaiming to everyone the truth about who he was.

❧

God, teach me to trust you and to believe that you are always working for my good, even when I can't see you. Grow in me a deep faithfulness like Anna's. May I, just like her, refuse to give up believing you, even if it means years of waiting and praying.

Day 3

Why We Don't Dream

You see things; and you say,
'Why?' But I dream things that never were;
and I say, 'Why not?'
GEORGE BERNARD SHAW

J*ust survive.* That's what many of us do. One day at a time, we trudge
bravely forward, but we don't really remember our dreams anymore.
We don't really reach up to God or out to others, and we don't engage
our hearts. We may stay busy, but we aren't really living out the destiny
for our lives that God intended. Sound familiar? In Joel, God gives a
beautiful promise of how his Holy Spirit can transform our "surviving"
into the abundant life that God intended.

In the Word
Read Joel 2 today and pay special attention to verses 28-29:

> *"And afterward, I will pour out my Spirit on all people. Your*
> *sons and daughters will prophesy, your old men will dream*
> *dreams, your young men will see visions. Even on my servants,*
> *both men and women, I will pour out my Spirit in those days."*

Yesterday, we mentioned that dreams are fragile. They can be bright,
clear, and strong at one point in our lives, but they can evaporate into
thin air if they aren't nurtured. Today, I want to be painfully honest
about the reasons women don't dream God's dreams. We'll focus on
three primary reasons.

Our dreams can be shattered by painful experiences. Tragic accidents, sudden disease, infidelity, financial reversal, and traumas of any kind instantly absorb our attention and crush our spirits. Even just one of these can hurt so badly that all we can think about is our pain. Our dreams seem to vanish. In place of the joy and passion of the abundant life that Jesus promised, we experience feelings of hurt, emptiness, and worthlessness.

If you haven't experienced this kind of defeat, you certainly know women who have. When we go through the most painful moments in our lives, we need a friend to walk with us—not to fix us or give us the best ten principles she's ever heard, but to just be present with us as we take one step at a time. Slowly, we will regain our footing and rekindle our shattered dreams.

Our dreams can be eroded under the sandpaper of negative messages. For many of us, our dreams fade for different reasons. Instead of a sudden calamity, we experience so much criticism and accusation that our dreams of making a difference become so much dust. Some of these messages may come from a spouse, an employer, or our children, but for many women, their self-talk is the most destructive set of messages in their lives.

Our dreams can be replaced with shallow, self-absorbed replicas that don't inspire or challenge us. Years ago, we had a passion to make a difference in people's lives, but something happened to us—life! The cares of the world. The pursuit of getting ahead. Gradually, we took on more and more responsibilities at home, at work, with our friends, and at church. Now we're so busy getting *good* things done that we can't even remember the *best* things.

Make It Real

Stop and think about it. In what areas of your life do you choose the *good* over the *best*? God doesn't intend for us to live this way! He wants each of us to have a dream for the future, to know that we can make a difference in this life, through the power of his Spirit working in and through us. It doesn't have to be grand and glorious (in fact, we should probably be wary of most of those dreams), but our vision for our lives needs to inspire and challenge us.

How have you seen trauma shatter peoples' dreams (in your own life, or in a friend/family member's life)?

What kinds of messages can erode our dreams if we pay too much attention to them?

Why is it so easy for shallow, immediate goals to replace God-inspired dreams?

Revisit Joel 2:28-29. What is the connection between being God's servant and receiving his dream for our lives?

How can you begin today to dream again?

Take a moment to read each one of these verses and think about how they apply to your life. Wherever you can do it, insert your name in the verses. Pray these passages over your heart.

- "Teach us to number our days, that we may gain a heart of wisdom" (Psalm 90:12).
- "Forget the former things; do not dwell on the past. See, I am doing a new thing! Now it springs up; do you not perceive it? I am making a way in the wilderness and streams in the wasteland" (Isaiah 43:18-19).
- "But I trust in you, LORD; I say, 'You are my God.' My times are in your hands" (Psalm 31:14-15).

Heart to Heart

God's purposes bring life and breath into every fiber of our existence. That's what Os Guinness concluded. In his insightful and challenging book *The Call*, Guinness writes:

> God calls us to himself so decisively that everything we are, everything we do, and everything we have is invested with a special devotion and dynamism to be lived out as a response to his summons and service.[1]

Dreams are fragile. Don't let yours be shattered, eroded, or replaced by something less than God's divine plan and destiny for your life! Choose today to believe God…and dare to dream.

*God, open my eyes up to the dreams you have for me
and give me the wisdom to know what steps to take.
Sometimes I get caught up in life and forget that you're
in the midst of every moment of every day. Rekindle in
me a passion for your dreams and desires for my life.*

Day 4

Hearing God's Voice

*Prayer...is a two-way conversation, and for me,
the most important part is listening to God.*

FRANK C. LAUBACH

In today's world of text messaging, fast food drive-thrus, and high-speed internet, life can get out of hand pretty fast. We find ourselves rushing from one thing to the next. Drop the kids at school. Go to work. Shopping. A quick workout. Meeting the bus. Cooking dinner. A soccer game. Piano lessons. Packing lunches...and on and on it goes.

"Be still, and know that I am God," the psalmist writes. And we have to wonder what *stillness* looks like. How can we hear God's voice? In today's passage, Samuel took time to listen...and God spoke to him.

In the Word

Read 1 Samuel 3 today and pay special attention to verse 4:

Then the LORD called Samuel. Samuel answered, "Here I am."

How can a woman know if an inspiring idea is God's dream for her...or just a harebrained idea? Good question! Sometimes, it's difficult to tell. When we think of our relationship with God, we can be sure of two things:

1. He is the king over all of his creation.

2. He speaks to his people.

All of us need training and experience in hearing God's voice, and sometimes we'll get it wrong. We may think God is speaking to us when really it was just the pepperoni pizza we had too late last night! I believe God speaks to us to share his dream in several different ways:

- Through his Word, the Bible
- By his Spirit
- Through his people
- In the circumstances we face each day.

When God speaks to us, it isn't just for our entertainment or a personal emotional experience. His purposes are vast and deep, and he wants each of us to join with him in touching lives. Whatever our dream may be, it certainly includes the powerful combination of humility, supernatural power, and God's direction.

We can be sure that *God speaks to us through the Scriptures,* but wait, not so fast! We need to learn some skills about how to read and interpret the passages we read, or we can get into a lot of trouble! Here are a few good questions to ask:

- What was the author saying to his original audience?
- What is the context in which the verse was written?
- How does this verse fit in or correlate with other similar passages?

God speaks to us by his Spirit's voice. This happens in my life far more as I'm reading Scripture and praying. As my heart is open and prepared, God whispers, "Go to the right" or "to the left." He reminds me of his love for me and for those I'm praying about, and as I ask him for wisdom and wait for his answer, he graciously gives it. Sometimes I have to wait, and sometimes I may not like his answer, but God is gracious and attentive to guide me when I need direction.

Make It Real

A relationship with God enflames our deepest desires and highest hopes. We come to him just as we are, but if we really grasp the fact that we have the privilege of a relationship with the creator of the universe, we are transformed. Spanish novelist Miguel de Unamuno understood what it means to relate to God:

> Those who say they believe in God and yet neither love nor fear him, do not in fact believe in him but in those who have taught them that God exists. Those who believe that they believe in God, but without any passion in their heart, any anguish of mind, without uncertainty, without doubt, without an element of despair even in their consolation, believe only in the God-idea, not in God.[1]

What about you? Do you just believe in the idea of God…or have you really experienced God? Do you know him?

When was the last time you stopped and just listened to God? How can you restructure your priorities and schedule to slow down enough to hear God's voice?

Read 1 Samuel 3:1-10. What are some ways we can know that it's God's Spirit who is directing us, not ourselves or the devil?

How do you know God's will? Has God used open or closed doors to direct you toward his dream for your life? Insight from friends? Promises from his Word?

Take a moment to read each one of these verses and think about how they apply to your life. Wherever you can do it, insert your name in the verses. Pray these passages over your heart.

- "But the Advocate, the Holy Spirit, whom the Father will send in my name, will teach you all things and will remind you of everything I have said to you" (John 14:26).

- "The Spirit searches all things, even the deep things of God…What we have received is not the spirit of the world, but the Spirit who is from God, so that we may understand what God has freely given us" (1 Corinthians 2:10,12).

- "'But let the one who boasts boast about this: that they have the understanding to know me, that I am the Lord, who exercises kindness, justice and righteousness on earth, for in these I delight,' declares the Lord" (Jeremiah 9:24).

Heart to Heart

Over the years, God has used some wonderful women to challenge me to be all God wants me to be. These godly friends have prayed long and hard for me, and in their prayers, God has given them words of wisdom to share with me. When I've felt discouraged, they've comforted me. When I've wanted to move ahead too quickly, they've encouraged me to wait and listen to God attentively. God has spoken to me time and again through these extraordinary women.

As I pursue God's dreams for me, he opens doors that I didn't know were there. But sometimes God closes doors that I've tried to open. Circumstances aren't a foolproof sign of God's leading or of him stopping our progress, but we need to pay attention to the situations in our lives and ask, "Lord, are you trying to tell me something in this?" Then listen.

Holy Spirit, guide me in your truth. Speak to me. Make my spirit sensitive to hear your whispers, and to respond rather than ignoring you. I want to know you, God. I want to hear your voice and experience you—not just in my head, but in my heart.

Day 5

Aligning Our Dreams with God's

God's gifts put man's best dreams to shame.
ELIZABETH BARRETT BROWNING

F ollow me. Those were Jesus' words to men and women of his day…
and to us. If we try to find meaning in the pursuits of the world—
possessions, pleasures, and status—we'll end up empty and miserable.
But if we align our hearts with God's, and we align our dreams with
his purposes, we'll experience more joy, love, and fulfillment than this
world could ever offer.

Our task is simple, but it's the most challenging thing we'll ever
do: to find out God's dream for us and to pursue it with all our hearts.

In the Word

Read Psalm 37 today and pay special attention to verses 3-4:

> *Trust in the LORD and do good; dwell in the land and enjoy
> safe pasture. Take delight in the LORD, and he will give you the
> desires of your heart.*

Many Christians have embraced a grit-your-teeth and make-the-
best-of-it lifestyle. They see following Jesus as primarily following a
list of hard and harsh rules. For them, the Christian life is drudgery.
Duty. Devoid of joy and laughter. But when I look at and follow Jesus,
I don't experience him or faith that way at all! Yes, there are certainly
times when the path leads up some steep, rocky roads, but I've found
that God wants me to delight in him every step of the way. Even when

I can't delight in my circumstances or the suffering I'm experiencing, *I can always delight in God.*

As I delight in him, I'm far more open to his leading, his correction, and his support. Pastor and author John Piper wisely observed, "God is most glorified when we are most satisfied in him."[1] To delight in God is to be satisfied, and, in fact, *thrilled* with his love, forgiveness, and purpose for us. As we know and love him more, we want to pursue his dreams, listen for his voice, and follow his leading, and we can take bold steps to do the things he has directed us to do.

The Christian life isn't a straight-line march. It's a journey of learning to delight in and follow God. Along the way, we inevitably take some detours, and we make a lot of mistakes. That's why I'm so grateful for his grace! If I wait to follow him until I have completely pure motives, I'd be waiting a long time. God is in the process of transforming our hearts, but they won't be spotless until we see Jesus face-to-face. Until then, I have to lean on him for wisdom, strength, and forgiveness. One day at a time.

Make It Real

When we follow Jesus with all of our hearts, an amazing thing happens to us: We don't have to look over our shoulder all the time. The nagging guilt that plagues some of us will gradually disappear, and the consuming selfishness that thrives on comparison and ruins our lives will be turned into thankfulness and heartfelt joy found in helping others.

There's nothing like it. Men and women who have found God's dream for their lives have changed the world—one person at a time. We'll never know the names of most of these people, but you and I know Jesus today because of their influence. God has used a grandmother or an aunt or a teacher or a friend to touch our lives. These people cared more about God and others than themselves, and eternity—our eternity—is different because of it.

What do you think it means to align our dreams with God's? Is that attractive to you? Why or why not?

Read Psalm 37:3-4. How does this passage describe the alignment of our dreams and God's?

I've waited until today to ask you to do this: How would you describe God's dream for your life?

If you can't identify a particular dream very easily, don't be discouraged. Think about your gifts and talents—those things that make you feel most alive and that help others. Then earnestly pray, and ask God to give you wisdom. Listen to him. Read the Word. Talk to a few friends and mentors that you trust to speak into your life.

Understanding what God has for you may not come like a lightning bolt, but more as a calm and steady sense of knowing. As you talk to God and listen to him, remember to "seek first his kingdom and his righteousness, and all these things will be given to you as well" (Matthew 6:33). *All these things*...including your dreams.

Take a moment to read each one of these verses and think about how they apply to your life. Wherever you can do it, insert your name in the verses. Pray these passages over your heart.

- "I desire to do your will, my God; your law is within my heart" (Psalm 40:8).
- "Yes, LORD, walking in the way of your laws, we wait for you; your name and renown are the desire of our hearts" (Isaiah 26:8).
- "Therefore, I urge you, brothers and sisters, in view of God's mercy, to offer your bodies as a living sacrifice, holy and pleasing to God—this is your true and proper worship" (Romans 12:1).

Heart to Heart

As we pursue God's dreams, we may need to realign our priorities.

This process challenges us to the core because it forces us to evaluate our deepest desires and ask God for clarity. It would be a lot easier if life revolved around our peace and happiness, but that's not God's way.

Dare to surrender your own dreams to God today and seek out his dreams for you. After all, his plans for our lives are far bigger than we could ever dream up on our own. When we choose to pursue God's plans for us, we'll sense his delight in us, we'll see God use us to touch other's lives, and we'll feel more joy than ever before.

There will come a day when we meet Jesus, and on that day, those who have followed him will hear him say, "Well done, good and faithful servant. Enter into the joy of your Master."

I want to hear those words, don't you? When we live out God's dream for us, one day, one decision, one moment at a time, even when it's hard, we are storing up for the "Well done, daughter" that we will hear one day.

Today and every day, as you hop out of bed and your feet hit the floor, ask, "Lord, what do you have for me today? Give me wisdom to see you and obey you."

One day at a time, each day full of faithfulness and obedience, until we hear those blessed words: "Well done! Enter into joy!"

God, show me the dream you have for me...at least enough for just the next step. Give me the faith to trust you, even when I can't see what exactly you're doing. I don't want my life to be just about me, God. Use me! I'm yours.

practice
stay in the prayer
attitude of prayer
treat people better than you treat yourself

"count it all joy"
teach me what you want me to do
for the

Week 8

Extraordinary Connections:
From Loneliness to Laughter

[connect:] to engage in deep, authentic, and meaningful relationships that change and shape who I am

Relationships matter. In fact, the people close to us are some of God's greatest blessings. We may spend time and money on all kinds of things—our hair, clothes, shoes, houses, furniture, pedicures, vacations, presents, and countless others—but the fulfillment and joy we experience is directly dependent upon the quality of our relationships.

As women, the desire at the core of our hearts is to be *known*. Not for who we pretend to be. Not for what we do or don't do! But for who we truly are. We long for rich, real, deep connections with God and people we can trust. We want friends who are committed to being there for us in the trying moments, when we need a shoulder to cry on and in the wonderful moments when we jump for joy. And they jump for joy with us!

Too often, though, we settle for something less than deep, lasting connection—superficial conversations, begrudging trust, holding people at arm's length for fear of getting hurt, and the illusion of safety by controlling others instead of loving them.

This week, we're going to look at Ruth's magnificent loyalty to her discouraged, grieving, depressed mother-in-law, and we'll see the value of honesty in Jesus' relationship with two sisters. In families and friendships, in our neighborhoods and churches and at work, the elements of love and loyalty define our lives.

He's closer than the breath we breathe.

Thelma Wells

Day 1

Forged in a Furnace

A friend loves at all times, and a brother is born for adversity.

PROVERBS 17:7

Imagine losing your husband. It is during a time of famine in the land and you are also filled with personal emptiness, hunger, and sorrow. You are alone. Discouraged. Grieving. Then, your mother-in-law decides to move back to her homeland. A mother-in-law who had loved you. Accepted you. One who came alongside you as a godly influence in your life. What would you do? In today's story, Ruth chooses to leave her people, her country, and everything familiar to her...and cling to her relationship with Naomi.

In the Word

Read Ruth 1 today and pay special attention to verses 16-17:

> *But Ruth replied, "Don't urge me to leave you or to turn back from you. Where you go I will go, and where you stay I will stay. Your people will be my people and your God my God. Where you die I will die, and there I will be buried. May the LORD deal with me, be it ever so severely, if anything but death separates you and me."*

Naomi had experienced tragic heartaches. Her beloved husband Elimelech had died. Then, a few years later, both of her sons died, too, leaving behind two foreign wives, Orpah and Ruth. To make matters even worse, a famine gripped the land. As she prepared to journey back to her homeland of Judah, Naomi realized she had nothing to offer these two daughters-in-law. She urged them to go back to their homeland of Moab and make a life there.

Orpah decided to return home, but Ruth made a different choice. Even in the face of Naomi's grieving demeanor and insistence that she leave, Ruth declared her loyalty to her despondent mother-in-law, and the two women traveled to Bethlehem. It was now Ruth's turn to come alongside Naomi in an act of selfless compassion.

In one of the most beautiful stories in the Scriptures, God honored Ruth as she honored Naomi. A distant relative, Boaz, recognized that she had special qualities of strength of character and devotion, and he married her. We need to realize, however, that Ruth demonstrated love and loyalty for Naomi when there was no hint of any payback. Her motives were as pure as snow. In the end, God rewarded this foreigner's love by putting her in the lineage of David, and eventually, Jesus.

Make It Real

I believe that genuine love and loyalty are forged in the furnace of heartache and suffering. These awful moments bring us to decisions: to take the easy way out or to remain steadfast in our commitment to another person, even if we see little hope of relief. Through the eyes of love, the relationship itself is the reward.

I've known many families who came face-to-face with sudden tragedy (such as a child's death or financial collapse) or chronic dysfunction (such as mental illness, disease, or a prodigal child). Sometimes people said, "That's too much for me. I'm out of here."

But a few intrepid, courageous souls responded like Ruth: "No matter what, I'm committed to you. Together, we'll work this out." The weeks, months, and maybe even years in the furnace of testing in a relationship may be the most difficult in our lives—and for a variety of reasons (mostly our own stubborn selfishness), it doesn't always work out. But those who come out on the other side have a purified, strengthened love for each other.

What are some "furnaces" you've experienced in relationships? How did you respond in each case? Did any of them produce something new and beautiful?

Reread Ruth 1. Be honest. If you had been one of the daughters-in-law, would you have been more like Orpah, who left, or Ruth, who stayed with Naomi? Explain your answer.

Ruth was a loyal daughter-in-law and friend. What are some of the rewards of loyalty? What are some limits of loyalty?

Take a moment to read each one of these verses and think about how they apply to your life. Wherever you can do it, insert your name in the verses. Pray these passages over your heart.

- "Two are better than one, because they have a good return for their labor: If either of them falls down, one can help the other up. But pity anyone who falls and has no one to help them up!" (Ecclesiastes 4:9-10).

- "One who has unreliable friends soon comes to ruin, but there is a friend who sticks closer than a brother" (Proverbs 18:24).

Heart to Heart

Relationships are hard work! Early on in our marriage, there was a time when I just wanted to run away. Understanding and loving Tim was just too hard, and I felt like the only solution was to get out. I left him, but he pursued me. The next few months were excruciatingly difficult, but in the heat of those conversations and the pain of facing disagreements and misunderstandings, God created something new and beautiful between us.

I wish I could say that all difficulties in relationships are easily resolved, but that's far from true. Sooner or later, we all find ourselves in the heat of strained or broken connections. When that happens, don't bail out too quickly. Stay in the heat for a while and let God forge something new, something strong, and something you can enjoy the rest of your life.

⌒

Lord, thank you for the gift of loyal, committed people
in my life. Bring true, godly friends into my life, and
give me the courage to be the same kind of person
in others' lives. Make me a woman like Ruth.

Day 2

Honesty, Even When It Hurts

*A true friend will tell you the truth to your
face, not behind your back.*

SASHA AZAVEDO

Fake. We all hate it, longing for friends who are open. Trustworthy. Honest, even when it hurts. Because when you and I hide our frustration and pain, it only festers inside. When we withdraw rather than talking things out, we put up walls in our relationships. Sure, we may paste on a smile, but, before we know it, our "friendships" have turned into little more than shallow chit-chat that leaves us empty, alone, and longing for something real. In today's story, Mary took a big risk by being gut-honest with Jesus. And Jesus didn't tell her to "get it together." No, Jesus cried with her.

In the Word

Read John 11 today and pay special attention to verses 32-33:

> *When Mary reached the place where Jesus was and saw him, she fell at his feet and said, "Lord, if you had been here, my brother would not have died." When Jesus saw her weeping, and the Jews who had come along with her also weeping, he was deeply moved in spirit and troubled.*

I love reading about the sisters Mary and Martha. Jesus had a special friendship with them, and he realized they were as different as night and day. When we think of them, we often think first of Jesus' encounter with Martha in their home. As Mary enjoyed spending time with Jesus, Martha complained that no one (that would be you, Mary!) was helping her cook for the crowd of hungry disciples. "Mary has chosen what is better," Jesus said. And his kind but direct words of correction communicate the priority of people over activity. This story serves as a model for how to graciously confront those who need a little attitude adjustment.

But I want to focus on a different conversation between Jesus and these sisters. In the last days of Jesus' earthly life, he and his men were camped several days away from Bethany, the hometown of the sisters and their brother Lazarus. When Lazarus became deathly ill, the sisters sent word to their friend to come back and heal him. Their faith was great, and their need was intense, but Jesus didn't come for several days. While they waited, Lazarus died.

When Jesus finally arrived at Bethany, Lazarus had been dead four days. When the sisters saw him coming, they ran to see him. They were deeply hurt by Jesus' apparent apathy and neglect. The sisters didn't mince words. They blamed him and didn't sugarcoat their pain. Both of them said almost the exact same thing to him—"Lord, if you had been here, Lazarus wouldn't have died."

We know the rest of the story. Jesus wept. He was grieved at the evil reality of death in this fallen world. But then Jesus raised Lazarus from the tomb and restored him to his sisters. This marvelous event, however, wasn't exactly celebrated among the religious elite in Jerusalem. Beginning that day, they plotted to kill Jesus. We could study the significant foreshadowing of Christ's resurrection, but I want to focus today on Jesus' relationship with these two women.

Make It Real

When we feel hurt, disappointed, and angry with someone, our first impulse is "fight or flight," to lash out or withdraw in silence. If we explode in anger, we may feel completely justified, but we tear down bridges instead of building them. And if we bottle up our hurt, fear, and rage, we may believe we're doing the "nice Christian" thing, but it eats us alive from the inside out, and sooner or later, the volcano explodes. Neither of these is a productive strategy.

I want to make a few suggestions about the importance and limits of honesty.

Be completely honest with God. In Psalm 62, David encourages us to pour out our hearts to God. Don't worry; he can take it. Express your hopes, fears, doubts, and desires. Hold nothing back. Let God into the depths of your soul. He delights in his children coming to him in honesty and sincerity, just like you want those you love and care about to come to you.

Be diplomatic with people. Don't explode or implode. Prepare your opening line. Ask for clarification and assume you misunderstood instead of accusing the other person of evil intent. You can say, "Maybe I didn't understand what you were saying. Would you explain it to me again?" And then you can say, "Here's what I'm hearing you say. Is that right?"

Begin with your feelings and your desires. Unless the person has proven to be abusive, begin difficult conversations with statements of feelings: "I feel hurt," "I feel angry," "I feel discouraged," or whatever your emotions may be. Don't ask the person to fix you and make you feel better. Instead, follow this statement with your desires, for instance: "I'd like for us to have a respectful conversation. We don't have to agree on everything, but I'd like for us to at least understand what each other is saying. Can we do that?"

Be realistic in your expectations of change. Most women are far more skilled in verbal abilities than the men in their lives, so don't expect your husband or teenage son to become an expert overnight. Look for progress, and be thrilled with any steps forward. Value the other person's genuine commitment, even if you still see room for improvement.

When you get frustrated or angry, do you lean toward the fight or flight response? What are the usual results?

Read Psalm 62:5-8. How often do you pour out your heart to the Lord? Does this seem attractive to you? Why or why not?

Look at the suggestions about being wise and appropriate when honestly expressing yourself in relationships. Which ones do you need to grow in?

Take a moment to read each one of these verses and think about how they apply to your life. Wherever you can do it, insert your name in the verses. Pray these passages over your heart.

- "Therefore each of you must put off falsehood and speak truthfully to your neighbor, for we are all members of one body" (Ephesians 4:25).

- "Do not lie to each other, since you have taken off your old self with its practices and have put on the new self, which is being renewed in knowledge in the image of its Creator" (Colossians 3:9-10).

Heart to Heart

We can't have real connections without real honesty that is salted with "truth in love." One of my favorite quotations about gut-honest relationships is by John Fischer:

> Real Christians are marked by sincerity—the whole truth about themselves and the whole truth about God. Real Christians stand before people the way they stand before God—transparent and vulnerable. Anything less is a dressed-up Gospel.[1]

God, I want to be honest with you. I want to tell you my deepest truths rather than pray to you like I'm put together or have my life figured out. You already know everything about me. Thank you for the freedom I have to come boldly before your throne.

Day 3

It's All About Love

*People need loving the most
when they deserve it the least.*
JOHN HARRIGAN

Years ago, a Christian group on a college campus advertised a seminar titled: "Givers, Takers, and Other Kinds of Lovers." We use the word "love" to mean almost any kind of connection today, but this leads to lots of misunderstanding. Needing someone isn't loving them, and controlling them by any form of manipulation isn't in their best interest. Real love is a choice, it's open and freeing, demanding nothing in return. In Romans 12, Paul dives into what it means to live out love in our daily relationships.

In the Word

Read Romans 12:9-21 today and pay special attention to verses 9-10:

Love must be sincere. Hate what is evil; cling to what is good. Be devoted to one another in love. Honor one another above yourselves.

Sincere. Devoted. Honoring. Paul used these words when talking about true, unselfish love. When you and I interact with other people, are we more focused on getting...or giving? In every healthy friendship, there is a give-and-take. We bear each other's burdens, walk side by side through the struggles of life, and share who we are.

In their book *Relationships*, Les and Leslie Parrott write:

> If you try to find intimacy with another person before achieving a sense of identity on your own, all your relationships become an attempt to complete yourself...The best you can hope for is a false and fleeting sense of emotional closeness.[1]

There are three Greek words that signify different kinds of love. *Eros* is sensual, sexual love; *phileo* is when we love someone because of their notable qualities or they do something to make us feel good; and *agape* is unconditional love, the kind of love God has for us. The first two include conditions; but agape loves in spite of the negative traits of the other person. Jesus said that loving people who make us feel good is no big deal. Even unbelievers love that way.

But selfless love is very different—and very rare. It reaches out to those who can't give us anything in return: the ugly, the annoying, the petty, the time-consuming, and anyone else who can be a drain on us. Jesus also said that showing love for the outcasts of society—the hungry and thirsty, strangers, prisoners, and those who are naked (see Matthew 25:34-36)—is a sign that we really get what love is about. Christ calls us to actively care for the unlovely.

Some women, though, have never experienced the joy of true friendship. They feel the pressure to "rescue" anyone who they interact with... to take control, be strong, provide a shoulder to cry on, but never let anyone into their own ups and downs. In contrast, other women "let it all out," wearing their hearts on their sleeves, without a second thought about the needs and struggles of other people. What about you?

Make It Real

We don't naturally love unconditionally. It takes a supernatural transformation of our self-absorbed hearts to produce this kind of radical love for unlovable people. We love, John tells us, because God loved us first.

The life of Christ can only flow out of us if the Spirit has filled us with his truth, grace, and strength. Jesus told his followers, "Let anyone who is thirsty come to me and drink. Whoever believes in me, as the Scripture has said, streams of living water will flow from within them" (John 7:37-38).

Who do you know who best models authentic agape love? Describe this person's attitude and actions toward the unlovely.

Read John 7:37-39. How does Jesus' statement here apply to his words in Luke 6 about loving, giving to, and serving those who can't pay us back?

Who is one person you can love unconditionally today? How will you do it?

Take a moment to read each one of these verses and think about how they apply to your life. Wherever you can do it, insert your name in the verses. Pray these passages over your heart.

- "Get rid of all bitterness, rage and anger, brawling and slander, along with every form of malice. Be kind and compassionate to one another, forgiving each other, just as in Christ God forgave you" (Ephesians 4:31-32).
- "But if we walk in the light, as he is in the light, we have fellowship with one another, and the blood of Jesus, his Son, purifies us from all sin" (1 John 1:7).

Heart to Heart

It's not enough to try to be "nice Christians." Authentic love can't be faked, at least, not for long. To love others with God's love, we have to experience his love in the depths of our hearts, let it seep into the crevices of our souls to heal our secret hurts and calm our hidden fears.

Then, with a full heart of gratefulness and grace, the love of God can overflow to those around us—even an insensitive husband, a selfish teenager, an annoying friend, poor people we pass by each day, and any other unlovely people in our journey. And in fact, we'll change our paths so that we come into contact with those who desperately need to experience a taste of God's amazing love.

John Bunyan wrote one of the bestselling Christian books of all time, *Pilgrim's Progress*. He knew a thing or two about the nature of authentic love, and he wrote:

> Christians are like the flowers in a garden, that have each of them the dew of Heaven, which, being shaken with the wind, they let fall at each other's roots, whereby they are jointly nourished, and become nourishers of each other.[2]

Lord, your love overwhelms me. Grow in my heart an unselfish love that truly cares about the people in my life, not just for what they can do for me, but as individuals with needs, hopes, fears, and desires. Give me wisdom in my friendships.

Day 4

The Fuel of Hope

*The need for fellowship is really as
deep as the need for food.*
JOSHUA LEIBMAN

Relationships are everything. I believe we are broken in relationships and healed in relationships. "It is not good for man to be alone," God said at the beginning of time. We were made for relationship, both with God and with other people. Meaningful relationships strengthen and encourage our hearts and fuel our hope when life is tough. It's nice to have someone to call when life isn't the way it is supposed to be. When the day gets long, we need friends who will give us a hug, share an encouraging word, and point us back to Jesus when we've lost sight of him in the midst of our chaos.

In the Word

Read Colossians 2 today and pay special attention to verses 2-3:

My goal is that they may be encouraged in heart and united in love, so that they may have the full riches of complete understanding, in order that they may know the mystery of God, namely, Christ, in whom are hidden all the treasures of wisdom and knowledge.

Academy Award–winning actress Celeste Holm remarked, "We live by encouragement and die without it—slowly, sadly, angrily." She was exactly right. People are starved for a word of kindness, affirmation, or celebration for a job well done. Time after time, I've seen Tim, my children, friends, and countless women who serve at our conferences light up when someone takes a few seconds to thank them or point out something they did well. Encouragement is light and salt to each of us.

We may think that Holm's comment is a little exaggerated, but it's not. Studies of orphans in occupied Europe after World War II showed that the mortality rate among infants not held by caregivers each day was substantially higher than the rate for those who received physical affection. For those children, care and affection literally meant life and death.

For the rest of us, encouragement comes in many different forms. In *The Blessing*, authors and counselors Gary Smalley and John Trent identified five elements of "the blessing" that parents can give their children: meaningful touch, spoken words, expressing high value, picturing a special future, and an active commitment.[1] However we define and describe encouragement, it makes a tremendous difference in our connections with people.

Make It Real

Everyone loves an encourager. Barnabas, the apostle Paul's friend, was labeled as that kind of person to Paul. What makes the "Barnabases" in relationships stand out?

They are intentional. These men and women recognize the power of encouragement, and they use their words and actions to make a difference in others' lives. Sometimes they comfort those who are hurting, and sometimes they inspire those who need a new vision. In virtually every interaction, they are looking for ways to build people up.

They are specific. I've seen the look on people's faces when someone told them, "You're great!" It was mildly affirming at best. But I've also seen the impact of targeted encouragement when a parent, teacher, boss, or leader took the time to articulate a person's specific gifts and the impact on others' lives: "This is how I see God using you," they say. Global statements are easy to give, but they aren't that effective. Specific affirmations make a huge impact.

They are creative. People who are gifted in encouraging others don't parrot the same things time after time. They find different ways to point out a person's strengths and picture a successful future. Creativity is important when you're relating to those you see every day—and especially those who are reluctant to receive your encouragement, like teenagers.

They are persistent. Encouragement usually follows the "law of the harvest": we reap *what* we sow, *more than* we sow, and *after* we sow. And we get lots of affirmation and love in return. But a few people resist our attempts to build them up. Perhaps they feel so much shame that they can't believe what you say about them, or maybe they are so angry they won't accept anything positive. When you encounter resistance, don't give up. These are the people who need it most! Ask God for wisdom to know when and how to touch their lives. Just like our children, everybody needs at least one person in their life who is crazy about them.

Look at the elements of people who are gifted in encouraging others. Which of these are strengths for you? Which do you need to work on? How can you take a step today to encourage someone intentionally, specifically, creatively, or persistently?

Who is one person who has really encouraged you? What did they do? How has it affected your life?

Take a moment to read each one of these verses and think about how they apply to your life. Wherever you can do it, insert your name in the verses. Pray these passages over your heart.

- "Do not let any unwholesome talk come out of your mouths, but only what is helpful for building others up according to their needs, that it may benefit those who listen" (Ephesians 4:29).

- "Therefore if you have any encouragement from being united with Christ, if any comfort from his love, if any common sharing in the Spirit, if any tenderness and compassion, then make my joy complete by being like-minded, having the same love, being one in spirit and of one mind" (Philippians 2:1-2).

- "Let us hold unswervingly to the hope we profess, for he who promised is faithful. And let us consider how we may spur one another on toward love and good deeds" (Hebrews 10:23-24).

Heart to Heart

Albert Schweitzer, theologian, philosopher, physician, and recipient of the 1952 Nobel Peace Prize, once remarked about the power of encouragement, "Sometimes our light goes out but is blown into flame by another human being. Each of us owes deepest thanks to those who have rekindled this light."[2]

Who has rekindled your light? Have you stopped to thank them? Whose light can you rekindle today?

Jesus, give me your eyes today to see the people around me who are hurting, lonely, or broken. Give me words of encouragement through your Holy Spirit to strengthen my heart and bring hope into the lives of others.

Day 5

Wounds from a Friend

Wounds from a friend can be trusted,
but an enemy multiplies kisses.

PROVERBS 27:6

Sometimes, true friendship means saying hard things. Confrontation is never fun. But all of us need people in our lives who care about us enough to say what needs to be said, even if we don't want to hear it. In today's passage, Paul discusses how to confront and restore a friend who has stumbled or is in trouble, which always demands "truth in love."

In the Word

Read Galatians 6 today and pay special attention to verses 1-2:

Brothers and sisters, if someone is caught in a sin, you who live by the Spirit should restore that person gently. But watch yourselves, or you also may be tempted. Carry each other's burdens, and in this way you will fulfill the law of Christ.

We all fail from time to time. David did. Peter did. And we all need someone who loves us enough to come alongside and help us see it. Oh, I know. Only compulsively controlling people enjoy confronting others. The rest of us can come up with a dozen excuses to avoid these difficult conversations: We're too busy, we don't want to offend anybody, we can't afford to get involved, we don't want the person to be angry with us, and on and on.

Let me make this very clear. It's not up to us to restore people simply because they have a "preference" that's different from ours. That's not a sin! But God calls us to "get under the rock" with people who are wrecking their lives. He doesn't leave it just to pastors or ministry leaders. If we care about the people around us, we sometimes have to say hard things to them. We say it in love, but with clarity and a strong hope for change. Unfortunately, the church doesn't always do this work well.

Sometimes, we need to look for a pattern of behavior before we say anything, but a few sins, like stealing or abuse, require immediate action. Before we go, we need to examine our own hearts. Paul tells us to watch ourselves because we, too, might be tempted. I don't think he necessarily means we'll be tempted to sin in the same way the other person is sinning. But we might be tempted to feel superior, to be controlling, or to demand compliance. To guard against these things, we need to be very careful.

Make It Real

When we do confront, it's important to be straightforward (not sugarcoating the problem) without being overly harsh. Paint a picture of the negative implications, but also cast a vision of hope if the person repents. We're not there just to pound him or her into submission.

Our goal is to restore, heal, and encourage. Ask for specific change, and if it's appropriate, set consequences for continued misbehavior. Consequences should always be age-appropriate, and they must be enforceable. Think about this well ahead of the confrontation, and have a reasonable plan. If possible, include the person in the decision-making. Quite often, children will propose more severe consequences than yours. This gives you the opportunity to be the good guy and ratchet them back a bit.

The initial conversation may be difficult, but it's only the first step. Remember, the goal isn't just to present the evidence or get a quick admission of guilt. The goal is repentance, restoration, and a new, healthy pattern of living. Stay involved in the process of growth and change. Offer encouragement and celebrate steps in the right direction.

Be patient. Change often comes slowly, and some people will test you to see if you really mean to follow through with the consequences. Don't be alarmed at this test of wills. Be strong, calm, and resolute.

Recognize the limits of your ability and your authority. If you feel unsure of yourself, get help from a wise friend before you begin, but be careful not to breach confidentiality. If things don't go well, either in the confrontation or the follow-through, get help from someone who has skills and experience.

Most of us can easily avoid the extreme of being a vigilante, righting every wrong we see in people's lives, but we need to avoid the other end of the spectrum: avoiding having the hard conversations.

Authentic love sometimes means we step in to speak the truth in correcting those who have gone astray. Jesus certainly did it, and if we call ourselves his followers, we'll learn to do it too. Jesus' goal wasn't to avoid hard conversations—he initiated plenty of them—but to point them to God for him to transform them and make them holy.

At what point is it appropriate to step in to correct someone? Give some examples of when it's appropriate and when it's not.

Reread Galatians 6:1-2. What might be your temptation when you confront someone in your life?

Review the principles in today's lesson. Which ones stand out to you as most important? How have you implemented (or will you implement) them?

Take a moment to read each one of these verses and think about how they apply to your life. Wherever you can do it, insert your name in the verses. Pray these passages over your heart.

- "As iron sharpens iron, so one person sharpens another" (Proverbs 27:17).

- "See to it, brothers and sisters, that none of you has a sinful, unbelieving heart that turns away from the living God. But encourage one another daily, as long as it is called 'Today,' so that none of you may be hardened by sin's deceitfulness" (Hebrews 3:12-13).

- "If your brother or sister sins, go and point out their fault, just between the two of you" (Matthew 18:15).

Heart to Heart

I've found that when I have to have hard conversations with family members, friends, or associates, they listen better if I first affirm my love for them, and then "hold up a mirror" to say, "This is what I'm seeing in your life right now." And I describe the specific attitude and actions, with the time, date, and place of what I've seen—it's not appropriate to be vague. And then listen. Sometimes I've misread the situation, and I need to apologize, but often, I need to listen as the person wrestles with the reality of pain that prompted inappropriate behavior.

Leo Tolstoy wrote, "What counts in making a happy relationship is not so much how compatible you are, but how you deal with incompatibility."[1]

God, give me wisdom and courage to know when to extend grace and when to lovingly confront and restore others in my life. Make me humble to accept confrontation, as well, from people who I know care about me. Thank you for using friendships to shape and change me.

Week 9

Extraordinary Passion:
Living Free from Secret Bondage

*[passion:] a desire to make a difference
in my world and invest in God's kingdom,
rather than just coasting through life*

What are you passionate about? What makes you feel alive? Do you know women who have that rare and attractive blend of contentment and passion? I know a few, and I love to be around them. It's far easier (and more common) for us to be on one end of the spectrum or the other:

- driven to prove ourselves by accomplishing as much as possible, burning ourselves out in the process,
- or hiding behind a façade of passivity to stay safe and avoid any risks in life.

The first group may appear to be very successful, but they are often empty inside. The second group is full of "nice" people who have lost their thirst to accomplish great things for God.

This week, we're going to look at one of the heroines of the Old Testament. Deborah stood strong for God when others around her had given up hope. And we'll visit a woman who encountered Jesus with her desperate need and wouldn't take "no" for an answer.

Passion and contentment doesn't just happen; it's the result of riveting our hearts on Christ, experiencing his love more deeply than ever before, and then being directed to "give ourselves away" to serve him and others. Along the way, we find that our culture's promises of success, pleasure, and approval may appear tempting, but can't deliver a full and thankful heart.

Think Clearly, Act Boldly

Wherever you are, be all there.
Live to the hilt every situation you
believe to be the will of God.

JIM ELLIOT

Confident, but caring. Bold, but not brash. Passionate, but also compassionate. An extraordinary woman isn't a pushover, but neither is she a drama queen. Deborah was a woman who trusted God and was not afraid to take a stand for him.

In the Word

Read Judges 4 today and pay special attention to verses 8-9:

> *Barak said to [Deborah], "If you go with me, I will go; but if you don't go with me, I won't go." "Certainly I will go with you," said Deborah. "But because of the course you are taking, the honor will not be yours, for the LORD will deliver Sisera into the hands of a woman."*

We are most alive, most fulfilled, and most effective when we have enough contentment to think clearly and the passion to act boldly. Deborah was a remarkable woman. She was the only woman who was a judge during the period between the occupation of the Promised Land and the kingdom, and she was also a prophetess.

Times were tough. A series of judges rescued Israel from their enemies, but once again, the people turned their backs on God and were dominated by foreigners. Deborah received God's directions, and she ordered Barak to take 10,000 soldiers to fight against Jabin's general, Sisera. But her orders didn't make sense to Barak. She told him to take his forces to the Kishon River Valley, but there, Sisera's chariots would have plenty of room to maneuver, and any advantage for God's people would surely be lost. Barak replied meekly, "If you go with me, I will go; but if you don't go with me, I won't go."

Fearless Deborah knew something Barak didn't seem to understand: God was going to do something spectacular in the battle. Sisera would think he had the advantage in the valley, but God would show up and give his people an incredible victory.

And he did. Deborah went with Barak, and God worked a miracle to rescue his people once again. Deborah commemorated this event with a song about God's wisdom and power. She was a common woman with uncommon faith in God's ability to speak, lead, and accomplish great things if his people would only follow his directions.

Allan Bloom, author of the groundbreaking book *The Closing of the American Mind*, observed, "Authentic values are those by which a life can be lived, which can form a people that produces great deeds and thoughts."[1]

Deborah's values were forged in the heat of her people's desperate needs, on the anvil of God's leading, and by the hammer of bold faith. When she became aware of the urgent need, she didn't panic. Instead, she trusted God to give her clear instructions. Even when others around her doubted, she stayed strong.

Make It Real

Our struggles today aren't with Canaanite armies threatening to destroy us, but we and our families face plenty of other enemies: distractions, busyness, temptations for our kids to get involved in sex and drugs, illness, strained finances, and a host of other very real dangers.

Author Richard Foster has a clear grasp of this struggle. He wrote, "Our Adversary [the devil] majors in three things: noise, hurry, and crowds. If he can keep us engaged in 'muchness' and 'manyness,' he will rest satisfied."[2]

Like Deborah, you and I can stand confidently in the strength of God. We can be bold and passionate about his truth, but also sensitive to the leading of his Spirit.

How can a woman be both passionate and content? How do these two qualities affect each other?

Look over Judges 4 again. What do you think gave Deborah the calm courage to lead her people?

What are the threats, enemies, and obstacles in your life today? How can you respond to them with passion...and contentment?

Take a moment to read each one of these verses and think about how they apply to your life. Wherever you can do it, insert your name in the verses. Pray these passages over your heart.

- "The LORD is my light and my salvation—whom shall I fear? The LORD is the stronghold of my life—of whom shall I be afraid?" (Psalm 27:1).

- "My soul is weary with sorrow; strengthen me according to your word" (Psalm 119:28).

- "It is God who arms me with strength and keeps my way secure. He makes my feet like the feet of a deer; he causes me to stand on the heights. He trains my hands for battle; my arms can bend a bow of bronze. You make your saving help my shield, and your right hand sustains me; your help has made me great" (Psalm 18:32-35).

Heart to Heart

An extraordinary woman stands up boldly for God's truth, but is also sensitive to the leading of the Holy Spirit. I want to be a woman like Deborah, who experiences the rich blend of deep, lasting contentment and a burning passion to make a difference for God. I want to think clearly so I can understand God's leading, and I want to act boldly to touch people's lives.

As you think about Deborah's life, what passions and hopes rise up in you? And what will you do with these gifts from God?

Lord, strengthen me in your Word. Make me bold to stand up for your truth, and sensitive to the leading of your Holy Spirit. Overcome the fear I feel with your perfect love.

Day 2

Holy Discontent

The truth is that our finest moments are most likely to occur when we are feeling deeply uncomfortable, unhappy, or unfulfilled. For it is only in such moments, propelled by our discomfort, that we are likely to step out of our ruts and start searching for different ways or truer answers.

M. SCOTT PECK

"But I have to...I just can't sit by and do nothing." Ever felt that way? A woman of extraordinary passion is driven to reach out and make a difference. Not out of guilt, or duty, but out of a genuine overflow of God's love and compassion in her heart.

A few years ago, Bill Hybels spoke at the annual Leadership Summit about the value of "holy discontent." He quoted the great philosopher Popeye, who finally became impatient with a need not being met and exclaimed, "That's all I can stand! I can't stand it no more!" (I can see him eating that can of spinach now!) Sometimes, that's the most good and godly response we can have to a problem.

In today's story, a Canaanite woman, who was a Gentile and viewed as a heathen, refused to give up hope. Instead, she sought out Jesus and persistently begged him to heal her daughter.

In the Word

Read Matthew 15 today and pay special attention to verses 21-22:

> *Leaving that place, Jesus withdrew to the region of Tyre and Sidon. A Canaanite woman from that vicinity came to him,*

crying out, "Lord, Son of David, have mercy on me! My
daughter is demon-possessed and suffering terribly."

Jesus traveled to cities all across Palestine. Sometimes he found
enthralled crowds eager to hear him speak, and occasionally religious
leaders challenged his authority. But one thing was clear: This man was
something special. The power of God was at work in him to change lives.

One day, a foreigner, a Canaanite woman (from the lineage of
people Deborah defeated centuries before) heard that Jesus could do
miracles. She had watched her dear daughter suffer for years from a
tormenting demon. When she found out that Jesus was nearby, she
searched for him, found him, and asked him to cast out the demon.

I can imagine the anguish and hope in this lady's heart as she
approached him. But Jesus' response wasn't what she expected. He
didn't even pay attention! Sometimes, God puts a need on our hearts
so great that we can't be content until God does something to meet
that need. So this woman persisted. She followed Jesus, imploring him
again and again to touch her daughter. Finally the disciples, clearly
annoyed, told Jesus, "Send her away; she keeps crying out after us."

Jesus turned to her and told her that his first priority was to find
"the lost sheep of Israel." With tenacity and grit, she got on her knees in
front of him and begged, "Lord, help me!" Again, Jesus argued that his
priority was somewhere else, but she refused to back down. Jesus told
her, "It is not right to take the children's bread and toss it to their dogs."

She replied, "Even the dogs eat the crumbs that fall from their masters' table."

Jesus must have marveled at her persistence. He told her, "Woman,
you have great faith! Your request is granted."

Make It Real

Holy discontent is the fuel for godly passion. Too often, we spend
our energies on selfish things, but holy discontent purifies our motives
and directs our ambitions to minister to the needs of those around us.
This kind of lifestyle isn't passive, and it isn't self-absorbed energy.

It's quite different. Writer G.K. Chesterton put it this way,

"Contentment is a real and even an active virtue; it is not only affirmative, but creative…It is the power of getting out of any situation all there is in it."[1] There are so many needs in the lives of people around us—excruciating hurts and pressing problems. How can we know where to invest our hearts and our energies? If we try to do it all, we'll either go insane or we'll barely touch people. Neither is a good solution.

To be focused and effective we need to listen to God's Spirit and get the advice of a trusted friend. We can't meet every need, but God can use us to touch a few lives. If we ask God for direction, he'll put people and situations in our paths and on our hearts. As we pay attention to the prompting of his Spirit, we'll dive in to help some, but we'll graciously say "no" to others. That doesn't mean their needs don't matter or that we don't care. It only means we can't do everything, and we're listening to God for his leading.

When we have this kind of holy discontent and God's leading, we can let go of guilt over the things we can't do for others. Because we're passionate about a few things, we feel energized. And because we're not spread too thin, we don't get burned out.

How would you define and describe "holy discontent"?

Read Exodus 18:17-23, the story of Jethro and Moses. What does "caring too much" do to us, our relationships, and our sanity? How did Moses change his approach to caring for the Israelites? Do you need to change your approach to caring?

Reread Matthew 15:21-28. What are some things in your life that prompt holy discontent? How is God leading you to meet those needs?

Take a moment to read each one of these verses and think about how they apply to your life. Wherever you can do it, insert your name in the verses. Pray these passages over your heart.

- "When he saw the crowds, he had compassion on them, because they were harassed and helpless, like sheep without a shepherd" (Matthew 9:36).

- "This is what the LORD Almighty said: 'Administer true justice; show mercy and compassion to one another'" (Zechariah 7:9).

- "He has shown you, O mortal, what is good. And what does the LORD require of you? To act justly and to love mercy and to walk humbly with your God" (Micah 6:8).

Heart to Heart

I'd like to tell you I've mastered this lifestyle, but I'm very much a work in progress. It's too easy for me to care too much about too many people. I don't think caring a lot is a tragic flaw, but it can lead to real problems if I'm not careful. Before I know it, I over-commit myself, spread my time too thin, and end up so exhausted that I'm not putting my whole heart into anything I do. For the sake of my family and my sanity, I'm committed to a life of holy discontent, with my energies specifically channeled by God's divine wisdom.

God, grow in me a holy discontent. Teach me how to delight in you and find my satisfaction in you, but not grow insensitive to the needs around me. Give me wisdom about when to say "yes" and when to say "no." Lead me to the people who need the encouragement and love I can give them.

Day 3

Consumed and Compelled

Some wish to live within the sound of a chapel bell;
I wish to run a rescue mission within a yard of hell.

C.T. STUDD

*O*bsessed. *Devoted. Gripped. Enthralled. Controlled.* That's how Paul describes what our response to God's love should be. So often I get consumed with the pressures and stresses of my life and I forget all that God's love really means for me. It's easy to start living for myself, asking God to bless my agenda and my plans, rather than giving every day over to the control of a God who knows every single last thing about me—and yet loves me with an everlasting, unconditional love.

In the Word

Read 2 Corinthians 5 today and pay special attention to verses 14-15:

> *For Christ's love compels us, because we are convinced that one died for all, and therefore all died. And he died for all, that those who live should no longer live for themselves but for him who died for them and was raised again.*

We all go through stages and phases in our walks with Christ. Sometimes we feel his presence so strongly that we are overwhelmed, but at other times, it seems that we're completely on our own and we don't have enough "bars" on our hypothetical cell phone to receive calls from God. Every relationship has its ups and downs, and we shouldn't expect our relationship with God to be linear. In the times of closeness, our faith is refreshed and nourished, but the difficult moments serve their purpose, too. They challenge our devotion and strengthen our resolve to trust him no matter what.

Ultimately, we may appreciate the many tangible blessings God gives us, but these can't be the foundation of a strong, lasting faith. There are too many uncertainties in life to depend on these. We are people of one heart and one mind, enamored with God's incredible commitment to us, marveling that he loves us so much that he has inscribed us on the palms of his hands. No matter what may go right or wrong in our lives, we can always come back to the one, true constant that is the bedrock of our relationship with God: the cross.

People who grasp the significance of Christ's sacrifice experience genuine transformation. They no longer value the same things, and they no longer respond in the same ways. At the core of their beings, a radical shift has changed everything.

Paul wrote to the Corinthians that the love of Christ consumes us and compels us. We are overwhelmed that Almighty God would care about us and sacrifice his life to ransom us from our selfishness and sin. The more we let his sacrificial, unconditional love melt our hearts, the more we want to honor him with every thought, every word, and every choice.

Jesus invited people, "Follow me," and countless have responded to him, but following him is the most rewarding *and* the most challenging experience life can offer. Author and philosopher Frederick Buechner wrote about the demands of following Jesus:

> God shows us a man who gave his life away to the extent of dying a national disgrace without a penny in the bank or a friend to his name. In terms of men's wisdom, he was a perfect fool, and anybody who thinks he can follow him without making something like the same kind of fool of himself is laboring under not a cross but a delusion.[1]

Make It Real

Paul described this transformation, this single-minded devotion, as appearing to be "out of our minds." Yes, it can look a bit odd to those outside the faith for us to love someone invisible, to sacrifice our selfish pleasures to serve others, experience contentment when others are worried, and be passionate about making a difference when those around us only want to climb one more rung on the social or corporate ladder.

How does being captured by Christ's love produce both contentment and passion in us?

Reread 2 Corinthians 5:13-15. What does it (or would it) mean in your life to "no longer live for [yourself] but for him who died… and was raised again"?

As you meditate on the love of God for you today, how does it shape the way you see yourself? Your time? Other people?

Take a moment to read each one of these verses and think about how they apply to your life. Wherever you can do it, insert your name in the verses. Pray these passages over your heart.

- "Then I heard the voice of the Lord saying, 'Whom shall I send? And who will go for us?' And I said, 'Here am I. Send me!'" (Isaiah 6:8).

- "If anyone has material possessions and sees a brother or sister in need but has no pity on them, how can the love of God be in that person? Dear children, let us not love with words or speech but with actions and in truth" (1 John 3:17-18).

- "God is not unjust; he will not forget your work and the

love you have shown him as you have helped his people and continue to help them…We do not want you to become lazy, but to imitate those who through faith and patience inherit what has been promised" (Hebrews 6:10,12).

Heart to Heart

To be passionate about Jesus is to know—to be convinced—that he is the supreme love of our lives. But this love is much more than a warm feeling; it's a deep commitment to please the one who bought us, adopted us, and loves us with all his heart.

We never have to wonder about his love. He demonstrated it—fully and completely—on the cross. The more I study and understand his love the more moved I am in my heart toward him. And for that reason, we live for him.

~

Lord, show me your love in a new way today. Compel me to reach out with the amazing love you have given me. May I be controlled and guided by your Holy Spirit, not just my to-do list. Use me today, Jesus, to love other people.

Day 4

Poured Out

Don't ask what the world needs. Ask what makes you come alive, and go do it. Because what the world needs is people who have come alive.

HOWARD THURMAN

When we give our lives over to God we "come alive" in the realest sense. We discover it's all about him and God accomplishing his purposes every day in our lives. Strangely, we find, like Paul, that in those moments when we experience God's love and pour it out, we experience the greatest joy.

That's why Paul could confidently say, "I consider my life worth nothing to me." Paul wasn't struggling with low self-esteem. No, on the contrary, he saw his life as fitting into a much larger plan—testifying to the gospel of God's grace.

In the Word

Read Acts 20 today and pay special attention to verse 24:

> *I consider my life worth nothing to me; my only aim is to finish the race and complete the task the Lord Jesus has given me—the task of testifying to the good news of God's grace.*

A friend told me she never feels more alive than when she pours herself out in service to God and people. "That's when I feel that my life really matters," she told me, "and that's when I sense God's smile." Have you ever felt God's smile?

Jesus didn't come to be served but to serve, to "give his life as a ransom for many." As we follow him, he changes us. We want to help others, not because we get brownie points, but because the heart of God begins to form inside our being. During the Korean War, Bob Pierce wrote in the flyleaf of his Bible, "Let my heart be broken by the things that break the heart of God." Later, Pierce started a new ministry to provide resources for the disadvantaged around the globe. The organization is called World Vision.

People can come up with a million excuses to keep from pouring themselves out to serve God. Here are some common ones I've heard:

- "I'm too tired."
- "I'm already doing too much now. I don't have time."
- "I don't have the right kind of experience."
- "What if I mess it up?"
- "I can't make a long-term commitment, so why even start?"
- "I'm too old (or too young)."

What are some excuses that keep you from being used by God?

Make It Real

Too many Christians find excuses to sit, soak, and sour when the kingdom's work is crying out for faithful and available men and women. Whenever I think of our excuses, I remember Caleb. He and Joshua were the only two of the 12 spies who reported back to Moses that they could take the Promised Land. Because the people trusted the other ten spies who counseled fear, God let them wander in the wilderness. A three-week trip lasted 40 grueling years!

During that time, the generation of doubters died, but Joshua and Caleb, the faithful two, lived to march across the Jordan with God's people. Caleb was now 80 years old, but he wasn't quite ready for a porch swing and a Social Security check each month. When Joshua parceled out the land to be conquered, the hill country was particularly well defended. Caleb called out, "Let me take it. I want that mountain!" No excuses, no whining, no taking the easy way. Caleb wanted to get the most out of life until the day he died.

Paul was just like Caleb. Nothing—including threats of imprisonment and death—could stop him from serving Christ with every ounce of passion and skill in him. When he was warned that his decision to go to Jerusalem would result in pain, he replied, "My life doesn't matter. All that counts is doing what God has given me to do." He poured out his life every day to please God and expand his kingdom.

When you think of being "poured out" in serving God, what feelings surface?

What's the connection? How does passion for God affect our desire for our lives to count?

Read Matthew 25:34-40. How does this passage relate to Bob Pierce's prayer?

Take a moment to read each one of these verses and think about how they apply to your life. Wherever you can do it, insert your name in the verses. Pray these passages over your heart.

- "Each of you should use whatever gift you have received to serve others, as faithful stewards of God's grace in its various forms" (1 Peter 4:10).

- "Anyone who wants to be first must be the very last, and the servant of all" (Mark 9:35).

- "Give, and it will be given to you. A good measure, pressed down, shaken together and running over, will be poured into your lap. For with the measure you use, it will be measured to you" (Luke 6:38).

Heart to Heart

God hasn't called all of us to become missionaries to the remotest parts of the earth, but he gives all of us open doors to touch people's lives. I don't know how God will lead you. I'll only ask you to think about the prayer Bob Pierce wrote in his Bible many years ago. Start there, and be responsive to God's nudge.

One of my favorite quotes about passion is by Sarah Breathnach. She wrote:

> The world needs dreamers and the world needs doers.
> But above all, the world needs dreamers who do.[1]

God has no greater plan than to use his people to share his love with others. Be a dreamer who is in touch with God's heart, and then take bold steps to change lives.

⌒

Lord, I'm learning it's not all about me—it's about you. Open my eyes today to the people you have for me to pour your love out to, and give me the courage to step out of my comfort zone.

Day 5

The Secret

There are many of us that are willing to do great things
for the Lord, but few of us are willing to do little things.

D.L. MOODY

The secret to a joyful, confident, passionate life is simply one word: *contentment*. But what does it mean? The state of being satisfied. Sufficient. Abounding. Enough. As women, a lot of us are worriers. Even as we seek to be used by God, there are a million things we can worry about: How is God going to use me? Will I be ready? What if I say the wrong thing? What if I fail?

But the reality is this: Every unknown in our lives is an opportunity for God to provide. And God *will* provide. Maybe not how we think, or the way we want him to, but God will provide. He's totally and completely faithful. And he loves to work in and through us.

In the Word

Read Philippians 4 today and pay special attention to verses 11-13:

I have learned to be content whatever the circumstances. I know what it is to be in need, and I know what it is to have plenty. I have learned the secret of being content in any and every situation, whether well fed or hungry, whether living in plenty or in want. I can do everything through him who gives me strength.

Much of the discontent I see in women's lives exists because we feel vulnerable, needy, and threatened—and we hate it! To keep from feeling this way, we put on masks to hide our insecurities, we try to prove we're valuable and effective, we go to great lengths to please people and to win their approval, or we withdraw from interactions to keep from being disappointed. Our culture has developed unattainable measuring sticks of beauty, performance, success, and possessions to let us compare ourselves to others. Comparison obviously sells a lot of products, but it robs us of true contentment!

The tension we feel, though, can be a window on our souls. Sara Paddison observed, "Stress is inner biofeedback, signaling you that frequencies are fighting within your system. The purpose of stress isn't to hurt you, but to let you know it's time to go back to the heart and start loving."[1]

I'll never forget a poster in one of my professors' offices which read: "Happiness isn't having what you want. It's wanting what you have." That's a paraphrase of Paul's secret of contentment, stated in his letter to the Philippians. Paul experienced the full range of life's events. He was worshipped as a god, and he was beaten and left for dead—both on the same day! He was a leader whose motives and methods were often questioned, but he never stopped loving God, reaching the lost, and caring for God's people.

The secret of contentment for this very busy man with monumental responsibilities was quite simple: He kept his eyes on Christ and he avoided comparison at all costs. When he enjoyed luxuries he didn't lose focus and drift into complacency. And when he suffered rejection and other hardships, he didn't pout, look around, and cry, "Why do other people have it so good and I have it so hard?"

Jealousy didn't steal his passions, and self-pity didn't erode his joy. But Paul recognized that this perspective wasn't natural for any human being—it came only from a close, loving relationship with Christ. Without him, Paul knew he would drift back into the pitfalls of comparison, but with him, he could "do all this through him who gives me strength."

Make It Real

The temptation to compare is so ingrained in us and society that we don't give up this bad habit very willingly. We cling to it until the bitter end. Where is that end? For most of us it's the point of brokenness, the place where we finally realize that playing the world's games and enjoying Christ, too, are counterproductive pursuits. Lord knows, we've tried our hardest to have both, but Jesus was right: No one can serve two masters.

When we get tired of it all, we're right where God wants us to be: open, honest, authentic, and ready to trust him to fill us with his heart, his values, and his purposes. Gradually, what used to entice us is no longer as interesting. Instead of worrying about not having as much as someone else, we may not even notice. And our hearts begin to realize that those things weren't neutral distractions: they were poison.

What are some ways in which comparison robs us of contentment?

Our thoughts are a window on our true desires. What do your day-dreams reveal about your true desires?

Read 2 Corinthians 12:7-10. How might God use suffering and other hardships to bring us to a point of brokenness so that we might experience true contentment?

Take a moment to read each one of these verses and think about how they apply to your life. Wherever you can do it, insert your name in the verses. Pray these passages over your heart.

- "Your father knows what you need before you ask him...
  Seek first his kingdom and his righteousness, and all these
  things will be given to you as well" (Matthew 6:8,33).
- "But godliness with contentment is great gain" (1 Timothy
  6:6).

- "Two things I ask of you, LORD; do not refuse me before I die: Keep falsehood and lies far from me; give me neither poverty nor riches, but give me only my daily bread. Otherwise, I may have too much and disown you and say, 'Who is the LORD?' Or I may become poor and steal, and so dishonor the name of my God" (Proverbs 30:7-9).

Heart to Heart

God uses his people, his Spirit, and his Word to touch our hearts and move us from worry to contentment. Thomas Merton was a brilliant student who enjoyed partying with his friends, but his life was forever altered by Christ's love. He described the difference God's Word made in giving him joy and contentment:

> By the reading of Scripture I am so renewed that all nature seems renewed around me and with me. The sky seems to be a pure, a cooler blue, the trees a deeper green...the whole world is charged with the glory of God and I feel fire and music in the earth under my feet.[2]

How might God use the Scriptures so strongly in your life that you "feel fire and music under your feet"? Every unknown in our lives is an opportunity for God to provide. And he will take care of us!

God, grow in my heart a deep-rooted contentment in the confidence that you are with me and that you will always provide for me. Keep me from comparing myself to everyone else, and instead, open my heart up to see what you see in others around me.

Week 10

Extraordinary Faith:
Believing God Even When
Life Doesn't Make Sense

*[faith:] an unshakable confidence that God really is
who he says he is even when I don't feel like he's there*

An authentic and extraordinary faith doesn't just happen. It is cultivated as we pursue God's heart and invite him to change us from the inside out. As we begin to see and trust him more, we experience changes in all areas of our lives—sometimes little by little and sometimes in sudden, dramatic fashion.

I love Jeremiah 29:11: "'For I know the plans I have for you,' declares the Lord, 'plans to prosper you and not to harm you, plans to give you hope and a future.'" But don't stop there. In the next verse God promises, "Then you will call on me and come and pray to me, and I will listen to you."

Are you ready to embark on a faith-venture? God promises to reveal himself to us when we search for him...like hidden treasure. When you and I see God, our faith grows. That's what this journey is all about. You and me, pursuing and experiencing God with everything in us.

This week, we'll look at two women of amazing faith: Abigail and Elizabeth. They trusted God even when those around them (specifically, their husbands) lacked faith. We'll explore what real faith looks like in every phase of life: the good and happy times, the difficult and confusing times, and even the painful, desperate times.

Refusing to Take the Easy Way Out

*When you can't trace his hand,
you can always trust his heart.*

CHARLES SPURGEON

How we respond to hardship often exposes what we truly believe about God. A woman's faith is revealed when a seemingly hopeless situation tempts her to give up. To give in. To stop trusting God and try to fix it all on her own. The hardships in Abigail's life unveiled her unshakable faith in God.

In the Word

Read 1 Samuel 25 today and pay special attention to verses 32-33:

> *David said to Abigail, "Praise be to the LORD, the God of Israel, who has sent you today to meet me. May you be blessed for your good judgment and for keeping me from bloodshed this day and from avenging myself with my own hands."*

Abigail had a very painful, difficult marriage. Her husband's name, Nabal, meant "Fool," and it seems to be an accurate representation of his personality. While David, the anointed and future king of Israel, ran from Saul, some of David's men had spent time with Nabal's servants and his flocks in Carmel. In fact, David's men had protected Nabal's shepherds and their flocks.

David's supplies were almost exhausted, so he sent his men to ask Nabal for help. Nabal's response was less than generous. He rudely told the men, "No way!" David was furious. He led his fully armed men back toward Nabal's house with every intention of killing him and destroying everything Nabal had. But Nabal's wife, Abigail, heard what was happening, and she intervened to stop David from this act of vengeance.

Who would have blamed Abigail if she had let David kill her "surly and mean" husband? I can imagine how hard life was for her, and now she had her chance to get rid of the source of that hardship. But she didn't. She quickly loaded donkeys with the finest foods in her home, and she met David on the road before he reached her home. When she encountered him, in humility, she sought forgiveness on behalf of her husband. Then she gave him the supplies he needed, and she pleaded with him to avoid bloodshed—not for her sake or Nabal's, but to keep David's conscience clear and his reputation spotless.

David recognized this remarkable request, and, blessed by her discernment, he did what Abigail requested. He took the supplies and left her to return to her obstinate husband. I wonder how she felt that night at dinner. She'd done what was right, but it didn't change her circumstances.

Then God intervened. In a few days, Nabal's "heart failed him and he became like a stone." My husband, Tim, always chokes on this story…because I tell him "don't mess with a woman who believes God!" After Nabal's death, David sent for Abigail and asked her to marry him.

This woman of faith trusted God and did what was right—and God honored her for her faith. While this story should not be taken out of context to argue that a woman should stay in an abusive situation, Abigail's sensitivity to the Holy Spirit serves as an example for us to follow.

Make It Real

Let's get personal. The tough moments of life reveal where we put our confidence. Like when the bills go unpaid. When we're worried about our kids. When we're afraid of losing someone we love. When our marriage relationship is hurting. You and I can choose how we will respond in moments of crisis and stress:

- *Will I take God at his Word and choose to trust and obey him, even if I don't understand?* (or)
- *Will I panic and try to take the situation into my own hands?*

Do you really believe God is there for you? How do you respond to trouble?

As women, we naturally like to be in control (or at least feel like we are!). But a woman who has put her faith in Jesus Christ needs to relinquish control of her life and her heart to him. To trust him. Do we? We trust God for salvation, but we don't always believe he's there for us, available to us, right here and now.

Think about stating it this way: I trust that Jesus will take me to live in heaven for ever and ever and ever, but I don't believe that he has any involvement in or power over the struggles I'm in right now. We often believe this lie—or at least we live like we believe it. But when we grasp the truth that God really does love us, is deeply invested in our lives, and is working for our good and his glory, we can make the daily choice to live out a God-ward faith.

> For Abigail, it was Nabal she wanted to fix. What is it for you? What are the relationships or stressors in your life where you have the choice between faith and fixing?

> What situations have you faced this past week that left you feeling empty and alone? How might Abigail have handled those situations?

Take a moment to read each one of these verses and think about how they apply to your life. Wherever you can do it, insert your name in the verses. Pray these passages over your heart.

- "Trust in the LORD with all your heart and lean not on your own understanding. In all your ways submit to him, and he will make your paths straight" (Proverbs 3:5-6).

- "God is our refuge and strength, an ever-present help in trouble" (Psalm 46:1).

- "Take up the shield of faith, with which you can extinguish all the flaming arrows of the evil one" (Ephesians 6:16).

Heart to Heart

There have been times in my life when I've wondered whether God is who he says he is. I struggled to believe that God loved me, in spite of my confusion and inability to completely trust. When my dad was diagnosed with an advanced stage of cancer, I didn't know what to do. Tim and I wrestled to hold on to our faith, and tried to accept the fact that Dad might not make it. At first, only one thought consumed my prayers: "God, heal him. I know you can." But as time went on and his health started to go downhill, I began to pray, "Lord, take care of my daddy."

Sometimes, my agenda doesn't fit into God's plans, but I'm learning to seek him and then trust him with my challenges. I have a sneaking suspicion that Abigail developed a habit of asking God for wisdom to cope with Nabal day after day. God answered her prayers and gave her authentic faith to trust him for direction when it really counted.

*God, I believe you...and I want to believe you more. I wish
I could reach out and touch you, to hear your voice so
I'd know exactly what to do. I don't have life all figured
out, and sometimes I have a lot of big questions. Give me
more faith to believe you and to cling to your promises.*

Day 2

Against All Odds

Faith expects from God what is beyond all expectation.
ANDREW MURRAY

Righteous women with unanswered prayers...I've met a lot of them. Women who continue to pray and believe even though the circumstances seem impossible. Elizabeth believed God was able to do the impossible, and God blessed her with a child in her old age, after years of public disgrace. This is a story that offers us more than a human model of patience and perseverance; this is a story of God's beautiful faithfulness to his children in ways that exceed human expectations and hopes. What an amazing God we serve.

When you wait on God for direction, peace, perspective, or purpose, you are never waiting in vain. He hears you. He cares about you. And he is the Redeemer. Hold fast to your faith and praise God in your times of waiting. He has not forgotten you.

In the Word

Read Luke 1 today and pay special attention to verse 25:

> *"The Lord has done this for me," [Elizabeth] said. "In these days he has shown his favor and taken away my disgrace among the people."*

Shame. Disgrace. Humiliation. In first century Palestine, infertility was viewed as the result of some tragic flaw. People assumed that the childless woman had sinned in some way that caused God to turn his back on her. But even in the midst of her pain, Elizabeth was "righteous and blameless in the sight of God."

Elizabeth and her husband Zechariah were in the public eye because he was a priest. Often, we put leaders on a spiritual "pedestal," and when their imperfections come out we criticize and gossip about them. I imagine this happened in Elizabeth and Zechariah's day.

Have you ever felt the ache of unfulfilled longing? Of being misunderstood by the people around you? Elizabeth must have watched countless other women experience the joy of having children. Her friends. Her neighbors. Her extended family. I'm sure she rejoiced with each one, but in her heart, she must have wondered, "Lord, what about me?" As the years went by, her age made pregnancy impossible. Still, Elizabeth continued praying and trusting God. That's not easy to do, is it?

One day, when Zechariah was chosen to perform a duty in the temple, an angel appeared to him and promised to answer their prayer for a child. In fact, it wouldn't be just any child; it would be a boy chosen by God to prepare the way for the Messiah! The old man, though, couldn't quite get his spiritual arms around the angel's promise.

Doubt crept into his heart, and he asked for a sign. After years of childlessness, I think I would have asked for a sign, too! The angel answered his request, but probably in a very different way than Zechariah had wanted. He made him mute until the child's birth!

The priest went home. I wonder what his first "conversation" with Elizabeth was like. He must have made signs, drawn pictures, and written out his account of the angel's visit. When Elizabeth finally realized what the angel had promised, her heart burst with joy, not doubt.

How did Elizabeth respond? Look back at today's focus verse. Her words are significant: "The Lord has done this for me." Elizabeth knew who deserved the praise.

Make It Real

Can you imagine? Though Elizabeth had never been able to conceive, she believed God. Just like that. Without question. I think I would have been more likely to say, "I'll wait for the pregnancy test results before I get my hopes up." But no! Over the years of disappointment,

God had nurtured Elizabeth's faith. Because she believed God was both capable and trustworthy, she had no reason to doubt his promises.

God doesn't always miraculously answer our prayers in the way we ask, but he always treasures and rewards our trust in him. I wonder how many times throughout her life Elizabeth begged God for a son, with no answer.

Our family and friends may shake their heads and say, "Oh, what's the use? God isn't going to do anything good for you. It's time to move on with your life." But extraordinary faith clings to God through the good times and the bad, trusting him even when we don't see any evidence of his Spirit's work, and even when family and friends have given up.

Elizabeth said, "The Lord has done this for me." God really is in the midst of it all! That doesn't mean we don't take responsibility and work hard to have influence, but ultimately, our lives are not our own. We are his. And we were bought with a price. The surrender of control brings tremendous freedom.

How do you cope with uncertainty when God doesn't seem to come through the way you think he should?

Read Hebrews 11, "the faith chapter." Can you identify with any of these people? How did "waiting" play a part in their lives?

What is one unknown in your life right now where you have the choice to believe God or give in to doubt?

Take a moment to read each one of these verses and think about how they apply to your life. Wherever you can do it, insert your name in the verses. Pray these passages over your heart.

- "Yes, my soul, find rest in God; my hope comes from him. Truly he is my rock and my salvation; he is my fortress, I will not be shaken" (Psalm 62:5-6).

- "This is the victory that has overcome the world, even our faith" (1 John 5:4).

- "When I said, 'My foot is slipping,' your unfailing love, LORD, supported me" (Psalm 94:18).

Heart to Heart

For me, the times of waiting on God for the impossible can be draining and discouraging. I so desperately want an answer that I try to tell God exactly what to do and how to do it. I want to hurry the process. And it doesn't work. If you're like me, you're realizing there's nothing you can do to fix and control it…whatever "it" is for you.

That's why I have to go to Psalm 46, and especially verse 10: "Be still, and know that I am God." No matter what is going on in my life he is in it all, even in those unanswered prayers.

Elizabeth chose to rejoice in God's promises, even when she didn't see God answering her prayers. We can wrestle our doubts believing the truth that "I the LORD do not change" (Malachi 3:6). He is faithful, merciful, and tenderhearted toward you and me. Always.

When we understand disappointment and suffering as tools in God's loving hands to grow and shape our faith, we can take joy in God's work, not just our circumstances. Difficulties don't mean that God has abandoned us. Far from it!

Lord, I'm growing frustrated and confused as I wait for _____ . I want to trust you and not give up. Help me, Lord, to sense and know your presence and your power. Grow my faith, God, and teach me what it means to really depend on you.

Day 3

Thanking God for the Good Times

God gave you a gift of 86,400 seconds today.
Have you used one to say "thank you"?
WILLIAM A. WARD

Gratitude fuels faith. How do you feel when you've cooked a wonderful dinner for your family and they wolf it down and jump up from the table...without even a "Thanks, Mom!"? Instead of expressing gratitude, they turn on ESPN or jump on Facebook. Sound familiar? How do you feel when you've spent lots of time helping a friend, and she seems to take your availability for granted? I think that's how God feels when we don't stop to thank him for his blessings.

In the Word

Read all of Psalm 145 today and pay special attention to verses 4-5:

One generation commends your works to another; they tell of your mighty acts. They speak of the glorious splendor of your majesty—and I will meditate on your wonderful works.

How often did David praise God? Refer to your Bible and fill in the blanks below.

Verse 2: "_____ I will praise you."

Verse 21: "Let every creature praise his holy name _____."

In this acrostic psalm, David uses immense creativity to speak out thankfulness to God. Each of the 21 lines begins with a letter of the

Hebrew alphabet. Tradition tells us that God's people recited this psalm every single day, along with the *Shema*.[1] While avoiding empty rituals, finding regular and creative ways to praise God helps discipline our hearts to ponder who God is.

Some of us face daunting problems that stagger us, but all of us need to ask God to give us eyes to see all the wonderful blessings he gives us each day. In our affluent culture, we take many of these blessings for granted. It's so easy to forget, to leave God out of the equation and act as if he doesn't even exist. Author Romano Guardini shows the absurdity of forgetting when he writes:

> How is it that God permeates the universe, that everything that is comes from his hand, that every thought and emotion we have has significance only in him, yet we are neither shaken nor inflamed by the reality of his presence, but able to live as though he did not exist? How is this truly satanic deceit possible?[2]

I often think of the story of the ten lepers that Jesus healed. Only one of them returned to give Jesus thanks. Too often, I act like the other nine men—I receive God's blessing, but don't pause to thank him. I want to be that one who remembers how God has rescued me. Who is overwhelmed with Jesus' kindness and love toward me. I'm committed to becoming like the one who returned. How about you?

Make It Real

Thelma Wells, whom I affectionately call "Mama T," often says, "Get your praise on!" God doesn't want a shallow "Pollyanna" sort of happy, but a genuine, thankful heart. Which kind of person are you?

- A *glass half full woman* tends to see the good in every situation and every relationship.

- A *glass half empty woman* tends to be analytical, realistic, and even cynical.

Let me say it again—gratitude isn't just a feel-good suggestion. Our spiritual health and our impact on those around us depend on our cultivation of this "attitude of gratitude."

Praise brings joy to God's heart (and ours), but that's not all. Praise grows our faith in God! As we look back and remember how God has been faithful in the past—how he has provided, cared for, and worked miracles in our lives—we can't help but trust God with the unknowns ahead. The more we see God working, the more our confidence grows that God really is who he says he is. And that's faith.

Grab your Bible and read Psalm 145:1-5 again. Write down some of the blessings and gifts God has given you and take some time to thank him for them.

Read the story of the healed lepers in Luke 17:11-19. Are you more like the one man who returned or the nine who didn't? How can you begin today to build gratitude into your life?

Get your praise on! Here are a few ideas to get you started. Add some of your own ideas at the bottom. Remember, *worship is your creative expression to God*, not an empty ritual!

- Make an ongoing list of things for which you are grateful to God.
- Carve out a block of time to thank God for answers to prayer.
- Journal, sing, dance, or paint in praise to God.
- Use your time in the shower, the car, or on a run to focus on praising Jesus.
- Post Scripture verses/quotes on your refrigerator, mirror, or desktop.

Take a moment to read each one of these verses and think about how they apply to your life. Wherever you can do it, insert your name in the verses. Pray these passages over your heart.

- "Every good and perfect gift is from above, coming down from the Father of the heavenly lights, who does not change like shifting shadows" (James 1:17).

- "When times are good, be happy; but when times are bad, consider this: God has made the one as well as the other" (Ecclesiastes 7:14).

- "When you have eaten and are satisfied, praise the LORD your God for the good land he has given you. Be careful that you do not forget the LORD" (Deuteronomy 8:10-11).

Heart to Heart

I recall noticing how the focus of conversations with my dad changed when he started his cancer treatments. Before the diagnosis we discussed vacations, dreams, plans for the future...all the joys that Dad and I were grateful for. But after, we celebrated things like his good blood count numbers, full nights of sleep, effective pain medications, and nourishing meals kept down.

Dad and I chose to praise God in both situations. We were just praising him for different things. In looking for the big, stupendous blessings from God, it's easy for us to get this praise stuff messed up. We forget the small, subtle, ordinary things that are also miracles.

These days, simple acts of holding a hand, watching a sunset, and calling my mom carry a deeper meaning than they did before Dad's cancer. What about for you? Take a deep breath and think about it, and you may just begin to see things a whole lot differently. I did.

⌒

Lord, so often I forget to say thank-you. I get busy or excited, and you just slip from my mind. Forgive me. Open my eyes up to see all of the ways you have been there for me...the ways you bless and take care of me. I want to invite you into every part of my life...

Day 4

Crying Out to God

To learn strong faith is to endure great trials.
I have learned my faith by standing
firm amid severe testings.
GEORGE MUELLER

Losing a job. A scary diagnosis. Sick kids. An accident. The list of possible trials goes on. We may not be stuck in desert wastelands or deep darkness, but it can sure feel like it at times. For the children of Israel, that hardship included captivity. Exile. Separation from their families. Living in a strange, godless land. Today's psalm tells the story of how God's people wrestled with adversity and cried out to God in faith.

In the Word

Read Psalm 107 today and pay attention to verses 4, 10, 17, and 28:

Some wandered in desert wastelands...some sat in darkness, in utter darkness...some became fools through their rebellious ways...Then they cried out to the LORD in their trouble, and he brought them out of their distress.

The Scriptures never sugarcoat problems in life. They tell it like it really is. Yes, we can have strong hope that God will somehow orchestrate even the most painful events in our lives and create something good from them, but the Bible never recommends minimizing our problems, excusing those who caused them, or denying they even exist.

On every page, we're encouraged to look at life straight-on and trust God's wisdom, goodness, and greatness. The process of being faithful in the midst of the struggle is where we learn life's most treasured lessons.

In Psalm 107, we find four groups of people who were in big trouble. Sometimes their dilemma was self-inflicted by foolish and sinful choices, sometimes it seemed like an accident, and in one case, God himself caused the difficulty they faced. No matter the cause of the problem, each group of people had the same response: They cried out to the Lord in their trouble, and each time God answered their prayer. Faith enabled the Israelites to believe that God was available and attentive to their cry.

Even when they couldn't feel God's presence.

Even when they sinned.

Even when they were confused.

Even when they were angry.

Even when they failed.

Again, they cried out to the Lord in their trouble. They were *desperate*. They knew they needed God. What did God do? (Hint: verses 6, 13, 19, 28)

Make It Real

When we encounter hard times or we are devastated by death, disease, or other unexpected traumas, we naturally turn to God and ask, "Why?"

What have you been asking God "why" about lately? Think about it.

- "God, why _____?"
- "God, why _____?"

"Why" is not a bad question, and it's not wrong for us to ask it. The problem is that we sometimes (maybe often) can't figure out the answer. So the second question we need to ask is, "What now?" No matter what the cause might be, we need to respond by clinging to God's hand and trusting him for direction. Sometimes, like in the story of Shadrach, Meshach, and Abednego, the Lord rescues us from our difficulties, but more often, he gives us the strength to walk through them. And when we are too weak to keep going, God himself carries us. Strangely, it's often in the midst of life's most difficult struggles that we grow closest to Jesus.

How do you usually respond to pain, heartache, and disappointment? Do you ignore it? Fake it 'til you make it? How do you cope?

What did the people in Psalm 107 do?

Desperation can drive us to do some pretty crazy things that only hurt us more. If you don't cry out to God, you will cry out to something else. Being a woman of faith doesn't mean detaching from or devaluing your heart. Rather than trying to push through and rely on your own strength, or just "cope," why not invite the one who is "a man of suffering, and familiar with pain" (Isaiah 53:3) into your struggle? Desperation should always drive us to him!

Take a moment to read each one of these verses and think about how they apply to your life. Wherever you can do it, insert your name in the verses. Pray these passages over your heart.

- "Out of the depths I cry to you, LORD; Lord, hear my voice. Let your ears be attentive to my cry for mercy" (Psalm 130:1-2).
- "Call to me and I will answer you and tell you great and unsearchable things you do not know" (Jeremiah 33:3).
- "I sought the LORD, and he answered me; he delivered me from all my fears. Those who look to him are radiant; their faces are never covered with shame" (Psalm 34:4-5).

Heart to Heart

I'll never forget that rainy, dreary, terrifying night. Driving behind the ambulance, my dad inside. The doctor had told us that day that he wouldn't live another two weeks. He was coming home from the hospital to die. Have you ever felt betrayed by God? I did that day. With a sinking heart, I realized the irony. *The next car I'll be driving behind is a hearse.*

As the tears rolled down my cheeks, I asked God a million questions. *Why? How could you? We asked you to heal him.* My heart felt as dark as the storm outside. I felt alone. Abandoned. Even angry. But I am learning that our pain is often God's classroom. Philip Yancey writes:

> Gregory of Nicea once called St. Basil's faith 'ambidextrous' because he welcomed pleasures with the right hand and afflictions with the left, convinced both would serve God's design for him.[1]

Do we really believe that God can fulfill his purposes through our pain? If we want his purposes and not just our comfort, we will turn to him in our darkest moments. Faith means truly believing, like Paul, "that neither death nor life, neither angels nor demons, neither the present nor the future, nor any powers, neither height nor depth, nor anything else in all creation, will be able to separate us from the love of God that is in Christ Jesus our Lord" (Romans 8:38-39).

⌒

God, I'm crying out to you because I don't know what else to do. I'm tired of trying to be strong and figure out life on my own. Just like you did in the Bible, I beg you to deliver me. Help me. Grow my faith.

Getting a Grip in Times of Confusion

Faith is like radar that sees through the fog.
CORRIE TEN BOOM

Fisherman. Disciple. Friend. Peter swore he would die with Jesus, if need be. Denying his master was unthinkable. And then? In the confusion and heat of the moment, Peter had done what he'd sworn he'd never do. He denied Christ. Chaos and crisis can wound our souls, tearing apart the faith that once seemed so real. Getting a grip in times of confusion can be really elusive. Like Peter, fear and doubt can lead us to do things we never thought we would.

In the Word

Read Matthew 26:31-75 today and pay special attention to verse 75:

> *Then Peter remembered the word Jesus had spoken: "Before the rooster crows, you will disown me three times." And he went outside and wept bitterly.*

Peter had such high hopes for his career because he was associated with and attached to Jesus. In fact, Jesus had told Peter that he was the rock on which the church would be built. What an honor! But now, at an awkwardly solemn dinner, Jesus was talking and acting very strangely. He said several times that he was going to Jerusalem to die.

Peter, like the other disciples, didn't know what to make of it. After all, the crowds were bigger than ever, and people were even talking about making Jesus their king. And if Jesus became king, who would be his Prime Minister? Who would be his Chief of Staff? That's right: Peter.

Jesus had always said some pretty strange things, like "The one who believes in me will live, even though they die," "Whoever wants to become great among you must be your servant," and things like that. But now, on the evening of Passover, he seemed very serious. Jesus predicted that one of the disciples would betray him.

Peter was startled. Wait a minute! He wanted to be sure Jesus and everybody else knew it wasn't going to be him. He insisted, "Lord, I am ready to go with you to prison and to death." I'd love to have seen the look on Jesus' face at that comment. "I tell you, Peter," Jesus responded, "before the rooster crows today, you will deny three times that you know me."

It was true. Early the next morning, Peter found himself telling a third person that he didn't know that man, Jesus. The rooster crowed and Peter realized he had betrayed the one he loved so much. He wept bitterly.

Make It Real

Ever had a Peter moment? In chaos and crisis, your faith wavered and you did what you said you'd never do?

There are times in our lives when we feel that we know exactly what God is going to do—and in fact, what he *should* do. We've prayed, we've studied the Scriptures, and we've talked to friends about the direction we plan to take, and everything looks like a green light. But somehow, things don't work out the way we planned. A child, a husband, a friend, or a boss doesn't respond the way we'd hoped he would. We redouble our prayers, and we're sure this time, things will go well. But they don't. Another setback; another disappointment. When we are confused, we may feel tempted to give up on God. In these moments, our faith wavers. Take time to pray, reflect, and talk to mature, godly people to get their input, but keep clinging to God, and cry out to him in the midst of your confusion. This prayer by Thomas Merton really challenges me to be honest with God:

> My Lord God, I have no idea where I am going. I do not
> see the road ahead of me. I cannot know for certain where

it will end. Nor do I really know myself, and the fact that I think that I am following your will does not mean that I am actually doing so. But I believe that the desire to please you does in fact please you.[1]

The rest of the story for Peter is that Jesus singled him out and met with him. In their conversation, Jesus forgave him for his failures and restored him so that he could be an effective leader. Confusion wasn't the end for Peter. In fact, it was a turning point in his relationship with Jesus. His faith grew! Not long after, this man who had denied Jesus was proclaiming, "God has raised this Jesus to life, and we are all witnesses of it" (Acts 2:32).

Think about that Peter moment in your life right now. You may feel confused because you're trying to trust God, but things aren't working out the way you thought they would.

Maybe your faith is wavering.

Maybe you're becoming jaded.

How can you apply today's devotion to your situation? Allow yourself to wrestle through the questions and doubts you feel. Maybe even write them out:

Jesus reinstated Peter after his failure and confusion. Do you believe that this same God will be faithful to you?

When you feel confused and frustrated, the promises of God's Word are an anchor for your soul. A light to show you where to step... one step at a time. When you find your mind wandering or worrying today, focus again on God's promises for you.

Take a moment to read each one of these verses and think about how they apply to your life. Wherever you can do it, insert your name in the verses. Pray these passages over your heart.

- "Because you have seen me, you have believed; blessed are those who have not seen and yet have believed" (John 20:29).

- "But you, dear friends, by building yourselves up in your most holy faith and praying in the Holy Spirit, keep yourselves in God's love as you wait for the mercy of our Lord Jesus Christ to bring you to eternal life" (Jude 20-21).

Heart to Heart

From the moment my dad was diagnosed with cancer, Tim and I began to pray for complete healing for him. We definitely struggled. And that dark, rainy night when Dad came home to hospice care, I just felt numb. I'll never forget Dad's words, though. He said, "Julie, God is going to heal me. Either he'll heal me here, or he'll heal me there... in heaven."

We may not always be able to "get a grip" on what's next, but we *can* "get a grip" today on Jesus. Hold tight to him. If you are his child, your Abba Father has you in his arms. And no one and nothing can snatch you out of his grasp. So keep clinging to the one who has proved his love for you, even when you're confused.

⌒

God, thank you for being faithful to me, even when my faith runs out. Continue to teach me what it means to really trust you, even in the dark. Show me the light of your Word, and when I can't trace your hand, God, help me to trust your heart.

Notes

Week 1

Introduction

1. Jean Kerr, *Finishing Touches* (New York: Dramatists Play Service, 1973), 57.
2. George Iles, *Canadian Stories* (New York: Choosing Books, 1918), 167.

Day 1

1. Pearl Buck, *To My Daughters, With Love* (New York: The John Day Company, 1967), 15-16.
2. Anne Lamott, *Bird by Bird: Some Instructions on Writing and Life* (New York: Anchor Books, 1994), xxiii.

Day 3

1. Vaclav Havel, *Disturbing the Peace* (New York: Vintage Books, 1990), 181.

Day 4

1. C. S. Lewis, *The Weight of Glory* (New York: HarperCollins, 2001), 26.
2. Lewis, *The Problem of Pain*, 116.
3. Nouwen, *The Wounded Healer*, 93.

Day 5

1. Mary Lou Redding, *100 Meditations on Hope, Selected from* The Upper Room *Daily Devotional Guide* (Nashville: The Upper Room, 1995), 8.
2. R. C. Sproul, *The Purpose of God: An Exposition of Ephesians* (Fearn, Scotland: Christian Focus, 2006), 40.

Week 2

Day 1

1. Anne Roiphe quoted in: Richard S. Zera, *Business Wit and Wisdom* (Washington, DC: Beard Books, 2005), 14.

Day 3

1. Stasi Eldredge, *Captivating: Unveiling the Mystery of a Woman's Soul* (Nashville: Thomas Nelson, 2010), 110.

Day 5

1. Larry Crabb, *Finding God* (Grand Rapids, MI: Zondervan, 1995), 18.
2. C. S. Lewis, *The Lion, the Witch, and the Wardrobe* (New York: HarperCollins, 1982), 146.

Week 3

Day 4

1. Gerald May quoted in: Luci Shaw and Eugene Peterson, *Water My Soul: Cultivating the Interior Life* (Vancouver, BC: Regent College Publishing, 2003), 121.
2. C. S. Lewis, *The Problem of Pain* (New York: HarperCollins, 1996), 91.

3. Walter Ciszek, *He Leadeth Me* (San Francisco: Ignatius, 1973), 88-89.
4. Dan Allender, *The Healing Path: How the Hurts in Your Past Can Lead You to a More Abundant Life* (Colorado Springs: Waterbrook, 1999), 5-6.

Day 5

1. Henri J. M. Nouwen, *The Wounded Healer: Ministry in Contemporary Society* (New York: Doubleday), 1979.
2. Daphne Rose Kingma, *365 Days of Love* (Newburyport, MA: Conari Press, 2002), 196.

Week 4
Day 1

1. Joe Stowell, *Why It's Hard to Love Jesus* (Grand Rapids, MI: Zondervan), 93.

Day 4

1. Frederick Buechner, *Wishful Thinking* (San Francisco: HarperCollins, 1993), 2.

Day 5

1. Philip Yancey, *What's So Amazing About Grace?* (Grand Rapids, MI: Zondervan, 1997), 84.
2. C. S. Lewis, *Mere Christianity* (New York: HarperCollins, 2001), 115.

Week 5
Day 1

1. Thomas Merton, *No Man Is an Island* (Boston: Shambhala Publications, 2005), xii.
2. Erik Erikson, *Identity and the Life Cycle, Volume I* (New York: W.W. Norton & Company, 1980).

Day 2

1. Catherine Mumford Booth, *Papers on Aggressive Christianity* (London: The Salvation Army), 67.

Day 3

1. Blaise Pascal, *Pensées: Notes on Religion and Other Subjects,* trans. Louis Lafuma (New York: Dutton, 1980), 172.

Day 5

1. Zig Ziglar, Ike Reighard, and Dwight Reighard, *The One Year Daily Insights with Zig Ziglar* (Carol Stream, IL: Tyndale, 2009), 324.

Week 6
Day 3

1. Larry Crabb, "Enter the Mystery: Heart First, Then with Your Head," *Christian Counseling Today* 15, no. 4 (2007): 58.
2. Crabb, "Enter the Mystery," 58.

Week 7
Day 1

1. Phyllis Stanley quoted in: Linda Dillow, *Calm My Anxious Heart* (Colorado Springs: NavPress, 1998), 105.

Day 2

1. Marian Wright Edelman, *The Measure of Our Success: A Letter to My Children and Yours* (Boston: Beacon Press, 1993), vii.

Day 3

1. Os Guinness, *The Call* (Nashville: Word Publishing, 1998), 4.

Day 4

1. Miguel de Unamuno quoted in: James Houston, *In Pursuit of Happiness* (Colorado Springs: NavPress, 1996), 264.

Day 5

1. John Piper, *Brothers, We Are Not Professionals: A Plea to Pastors for Radical Ministry* (Nashville: B&H Books, 2002), 45.

Week 8
Day 2

1. John Fischer, *Real Christians Don't Dance!* (Bloomington, MN: Bethany House Publishers, 1988), 51.

Day 3

1. Les Parrott and Leslie Parrott, *Relationships* (Grand Rapids, MI: Zondervan, 1998), 20.
2. John Bunyan, *The Works of John Bunyan: Experimental, Doctrinal, and Practical* (London: Blackie & Son, 1850), 570.

Day 4

1. Gary Smalley and John Trent, *The Blessing* (New York: Simon & Schuster, 1986).
2. Albert Schweitzer quoted in: Jamie Miller, *Yes, There Is Something You Can Do: 150 Prayers, Poems, and Meditations for Times of Need* (Gloucester, MA: Fair Winds Press), 13.

Day 5

1. Leo Tolstoy quoted in: M. Gary Neuman, *Emotional Infidelity: How to Affair-Proof Your Marriage and 10 Other Secrets to a Great Relationship* (New York: Three Rivers Press, 2002), 96.

Week 9
Day 1

1. Allan Bloom, *The Closing of the American Mind* (New York: Simon & Schuster, 1987), 201.
2. Richard Foster, *Celebration of Discipline: The Path to Spiritual Growth* (New York: HarperCollins, 1978), 15.

Day 2

1. G. K. Chesterton, *A Miscellany of Men* (Norfolk, VA: IHS Press, 2004), 159-60.

Day 3

1. Frederick Buechner, *Wishful Thinking* (San Francisco: HarperCollins, 1993), 28.

Day 4

1. Sarah Ban Breathnach, *Simple Abundance: A Daybook of Comfort and Joy* (New York: Hachette Book Group, 1995), 45.

Day 5

1. Sara Paddison quoted in: Michael Olpin and Margie Hesson, *Stress Management for Life: A Research-Based Experimental Approach* (Belmont, CA: Wadsworth, 2009), 256.
2. Thomas Merton, *The Sign of Jonas* (San Diego: Harcourt, 1981), 215-16.

Week 10
Day 3

1. The *Shema* is a centerpiece of Jewish prayers, recited in the morning and evening. It is based on Deuteronomy 6:4: "Hear, O Israel: The LORD our God, the LORD is one."
2. Romano Guardini, *The Lord* (Chicago: Regnery Gateway, 1996), 246.

Day 4

1. Philip Yancey, *Reaching for the Invisible God* (Grand Rapids, MI: Zondervan, 2000) 69.

Day 5

1. Thomas Merton, *Thoughts in Solitude* (Garden City, NJ: Image/Doubleday, 1968) 81.

About the Author

Julie Clinton, MAd, MBA, is president of Extraordinary Women and host of EWomen conferences all across America. She is the author of several books including *A Woman's Path to Emotional Freedom, 10 Things You Aren't Telling Him,* and *Extraordinary Women.* She is passionate about seeing women live out their dreams by finding their freedom in Christ. Julie and her husband, Tim, live in Virginia with their children, Megan and Zach.

Other Books by Julie Clinton

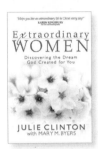

Extraordinary Women

Julie Clinton shares biblical illustrations, life examples, and prayers throughout this book, now in trade paper. Women learn to embrace extraordinary living when they discover God's dream for them, make every day count in surprising ways, and release control to take hold of God's freedom.

Living God's Dream for You

Julie Clinton shares devotions rich with wisdom gained through her ministry, life, marriage, and faith. Her message inspires women to grab hold of God's dream for them as they discover the depth of Jesus' love, the wonder of their worth, and the joy of walking in His purpose.

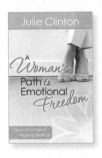

A Woman's Path to Emotional Freedom

Julie Clinton has met thousands of women desperate to break free of the emotional bondage of the past—the guilt, the anger, the jealousy, and the sadness. Julie offers women God's hope, freedom, and forgiveness.

10 Things You Aren't Telling Him

With encouraging examples from her marriage and those of women surveyed, author and speaker Julie Clinton models intimacy solutions to help a woman have important conversations with her husband about her hurts, past secrets, sexual needs, dreams and goals, spiritual needs, and her hopes for the marriage.